Registered by Custodian *asm* 22/5/42

The Bearer, whose photograph and specimen of signature appear hereon, has been duly registered in compliance with provisions of Order-in-Council P. C. 117.

Vancouver

(Date) March 10 1941.

JAPANESE NATIONAL

INSPECTOR R.C.M.P.

Printed by Britannia Printers Limited, Toronto, Canada

ISSEI

Stories of Japanese Canadian Pioneers

Gordon G Nakayama

Preface by Joy Kogawa

This is a Kagami Book

NC Press Limited
Toronto, 1984

Second revised edition, May 1984

All enquiries concerning the content of this book should be addressed to

Kagami
1063 Pape Avenue
Toronto, Ontario, Canada M4K 3W4

Canadian Cataloguing in Publication Data

Nakayama, Gordon G.
  Issei: Stories of Japanese Canadian Pioneers

ISBN: 0-920053-34-3

1. Japanese Canadians — Biography. I Title
FC106.J3N34 1984 971'.004956 C84-098470-7
F1035.J3N34 1984

We would like to thank the Ontario Arts Council and the Canada Council for their assistance in the production of this book.

New Canada Publications, a division of NC Press Limited, Box 4010, Station A, Toronto, Ontario, Canada, M5W 1H8

Printed and bound in Canada

Contents

Preface

There is today in the post-Auschwitz, post-Hiroshima world, much evidence for hope. The energy within the State of Israel, within feminism, within the peace movement, within the Christian church in Latin America – points to a new consciousness of social accountability. We have a new and vigorous perception of power with responsibility.

This hope exists simultaneously with the despair that as a species we are morally bankrupt and congenitally blind. Errors in history persist in our present world and in our own hearts.

With both hope and despair beckoning us, we Japanese Canadians today in 1983 stand at the centre of a crossroads. We are presented with both political and personal challenges as Canadian society slowly wakens to an awareness of its own blindness regarding the fate of Japanese Canadians during World War II. That awareness of blindness – a prerequisite of sight – calls us to examine our own possible blindness to sources of our courage and our renewal, both in our present and in our past.

In reading my father's manuscript, *Issei,* I have seen the evidence of enormous vitality in the lives of the Issei. That which was present to them is, I believe, no less available to us today.

I do not wish to romanticize the Issei but to humbly and gratefully acknowledge what it was that shone with such deep energy through their lives – in their hands, in their silences, in the earnestness of their intentions. That which was so alive in their blood and flesh and bones, that which moved them beyond and beyond their humiliations, that which was the source of their dignity, endurance and faith, is still with us.

I believe that we would do well, not simply to honour and acknowledge the Issei, not simply to hasten to give them physical comfort in their last days – but to see what it was that so informed their passionate love for us and to drink

7

from that same fountain. Therein lies hope – for us, our children and communities.

In many of these stories we can see that the Issei reached out with generous strong arms filled with gifts for their community and even for those who saw them as enemies. They did not 'see' the enemy. Some will judge their unseeing as a peculiar affliction – a false and dangerous innocence. But in my view, that vision enabled the Issei to escape the full power of the enemy whose greatest victory over our souls is in being defined as our enemy – as not-one with us.

It seems to me quite true that we participate in the creation of our realities. We often create the enemy by seeing the enemy. And we create the friend by seeing the friend. It takes two to make an enemy. It takes one to move towards reconciliation.

The Issei created friends for us among those who saw us as enemies, by persisting in seeing the face of the friend even when it was not there. That capacity to transform a broken reality and to make it whole can only come from strength – the most deeply powerful spiritual strength available to us, superseding all political power.

The Imais who gave away their land, the Shimizus who gave trees – these were not acts of folly, but the evidence of power.

Some will argue that without political power, our generosity is only servility or of no account and that true generosity cannot exist without mutuality. Our basic responsibility now, they will say, is to attain power.

But history teaches us that when lives are caught up in the scramble for power, we are in danger of being lured away from the sources of our compassion – seduced by self aggrandizement or causes made empty by being bereft of principles.

I pray that as a community we will not lose sight of the dangers, and that we will confront the challenges now facing us with all the spiritual courage to which we are heir. Generosity is our birthright. Through generosity, especially in our relations towards one another, we can be strengthened to engage in a dialogue with our fellow Canadians on whom the burden of our history also falls. With them we can strive towards the ideal of equality in this country where that ideal is espoused.

I pray that we will thrust ourselves from our complacency and insecurities and move for healing, thereby discovering the great wellsprings that can yet transform what we fear in ourselves, in each other and in the world.

The stories in this book are written in a simple, homespun style – thin biographical sketches of just a few of our many outstanding Issei. They remind me of some hand-carved wooden brooches I had as a child in Slocan – small home-made treasures – barely a handful of ornaments to bring to the vast, almost empty treasury where our stories belong.

Written primarily by my father about people he's known, or by others about those they have loved, these stories provide the barest of glimpses into the patterns, the community and the quality of Issei life. Dad gathered the material, interviewed and wrote the articles in 1981 and 1982. That we have them now in this form is due to the support of the Multiculturalism Directorate of the Secretary of State, and the dedication of Toshi Oikawa who assisted in editing, verifying, typing and shepherding the material to completion. Thanks are also due to Momoye Sugiman who helped edit, to Linda Ohama McLean and Nancy Suzuki for their assistance in typing and special thanks to Stan Shikatani for cover design and layout.

September, 1983   Joy Kogawa

Nakayama Family

Mrs. Lois Masui Nakayama, Timothy Makoto,
Mr. Gordon Goichi Nakayama, Joy Nozomi.

Introduction

There is a parable recorded in the Bible of a woman who had ten silver coins and lost one. She searched and searched and when she finally found it, she was filled with great happiness. I was reminded of this story when I was considering writing the short biographies of some of Canada's pioneer Issei. How sad it would be, I thought, if the stories were lost. And how few people know about the Issei in Canada. Yet how much more precious than all the silver coins in the world is each person's life.

Most of the people mentioned in this book are personally known to me. Some, such as my aunt and uncle-in-law, Rev. and Mrs. Akagawa, and Dr. and Mrs. Kozo Shimotakahara who called me to Canada have been very important in my life. Others are close and dear friends.

Both couples, the Akagawas and Shimotakaharas passed away some time ago, as well as Mr. Kiyosuke Iwabuchi, Mr. Eiichi Kuwabara, Mr. Shiro Koga, Mr. and Mrs. Denbei Kobayashi, Mr. Zenkichi Shimbashi, Mr. Genzo Kitagawa, Mr. and Mrs. Fred Masuyei Tamagi, Mr. Ichijuro P. Matsumoto, Mr. Takaichi Umezuki, Mr. and Mrs. Yasutaro Yamaga and Mr. and Mrs. Jiro Inouye.

The fact is that we are not here forever. Before I could finish the article on Mr. Thomas Kakinuma, the ceramic artist, he died of cancer. Then too, I visited 93-year-old Mr. Takuzo Maehara at his home in Kelowna in March, 1982. He was suffering from a slight stroke but was able to tell me of his interesting life. Two months later when I visited Kelowna again, he was gone. And my old dear friend, Mr. Shotaro Shimizu, 96 years old and blind, was visiting his son Dr. Kenneth Shimizu in Burnaby. I interviewed him there. Two months later, he died. I felt strongly how important it was to hear the stories of the Issei while we are still alive. (Mrs. Shimbashi of Alberta and Mr. and Mrs. Sato of Vancouver died in May, 1983 before this book could be published.)

Someone suggested that I introduce myself as well, so I will tell you briefly of my life.

11

I was born on November 16, 1900 in the small mountain village of Kurakawa, Ozu, Ehime-ken Japan to a farmer's family. We belonged to the Buddhist faith. When I was fourteen, my father passed away and I went to the ancient capital of Kyoto, where I studied and earned my living. I graduated from Ryoyogakuen High School and entered Ritsumeikan University in 1918.

In 1919 I came to Canada and worked at the office of Dr. Kozo Shimotakahara. I was converted to Christianity on Good Friday in 1920 and baptized on September 5 the same year. I attended Britannia High School and McLean High School at Maple Ridge, B.C. for a short time; taught Japanese Language Schools at Haney, B.C. and Fairview in Vancouver for eight years; married Masui Lois Yao a missionary teacher of the Anglican Japanese Church in Vancouver in 1926; attended Vancouver Bible School for three years and in 1929 entered the Anglican Theological College of B.C. (now the School of Theology.) I was ordained as deacon in 1932 and as priest in 1934 the year I graduated from the college. From 1929 to 1942 I pastored the Church of the Ascension Vancouver and during the Second World War, I served at Slocan City, B.C. and area, where there were about 7,000 evacuees.

Right after the Second World War, we were sent by the Anglican Church to start a mission in Southern Alberta where there were 4,200 Japanese evacuees engaged on sugar beet farms. We chose Coaldale as our centre and established the parish Church of the Ascension. From 1945 I served for thirty-three years as vicar of the church to both Japanese and Occidentals. In 1978 I was called by the Church of the Holy Cross, the Japanese Anglican Church in Vancouver to help them until the arrival of a new priest from Japan. In 1979 I retired after serving for fifty years in the Anglican Church in Canada.

Now I am enjoying a quiet life with my wife Lois Masui in our home in Vancouver.

If you ask me why I came to Canada I must answer simply that my father used to say, "Japan is a small country

12

and there are too many people. Some day one of our children may go to some other big country." When I was studying at Ritsumeikan University I remembered my father's thoughts, so I came to Canada where my aunt Mrs. Yasuno Akagawa lived with her husband, Rev. Yoshimitsu Akagawa. My aspiration was to become a medical doctor, but other plans awaited me and instead, I became a minister.

I hope this book will help in some small way to encourage us in our lives and to help us to remember some of the wonderful qualities of generosity, kindness, endurance, industriousness and faith which the Issei have shown in their lives.

I hope too, that like the woman searching for the lost coin, we will seek the valuable lessons and wisdom that are still waiting to be found in the lives and stories of so many other Issei — those who are still alive and those whom we remember.

December, 1982   Gordon G. Nakayama
                                            845 Semlin Dr.,
                                            Vancouver, B.C.
                                            V5L 4J6

Nagano Family Portrait 1910

Tatsuo George, Frank Teruma
Seki Uchiki (Mrs. George), Manzo
and second wife Toyoko Ishii

Manzo Nagano
First Japanese Pioneer in Canada

Manzo Nagano is reported to be the first Japanese pioneer registered in Canada. The story that follows was written by his grandson, Paul Nagano, a Baptist minister in Seattle, Washington.

Filled with adventure and dreams of the new world, a young lad, the fourth son of Kihei Nagano, begged the captain of a vessel headed for the West to allow him to work on board the ship. He, Manzo Nagano, never dreamed at that time, that he would be the first Japanese to settle in Canada.

Leaving Nagasaki in March 1877, the ship made its way to Yokohama, Japan, and then across the wide expanse of the Pacific Ocean to Victoria, Canada. Manzo was then 24 years of age, having been born on November 26, 1853. When the ship landed in Victoria, whether deliberately or accidentally, Manzo drove his stakes deep in the Canadian soil. Reflections from the past relate stories of Manzo, who, left alone in Victoria, was found hiding in the trees, possibly to avoid being transported back to Japan. After the ship set sail, he came out of his secret hiding place and was befriended by the Indians who had settled in that part of Canada.

The Chinese settled in Victoria before the Japanese, and Manzo mingled among them and sought employment. He worked his way up to become a foreman among the Canadian Railroad laborers. After most of the railroad employment ceased, the Asians had to shift for themselves. Manzo, having come from a fishing country, went into fishing; first working in a salmon cannery, then later in partnership with an Italian fisherman, entering into the fishing industry. He was very enterprizing and with his adventurous spirit, was not afraid to tackle new opportunities.

Seeing the need for a hotel for the laborers as well as the early arrivals from Japan, he purchased a hotel and became a welcoming committee of one for the growing immigrants of Japan. He would help them get settled in the new land. It is said that Manzo became somewhat of a mayor of the Japanese settlement, feeling responsible for his fellow countrymen. It is reported by one of his early friends that Manzo visited him when he was ill and comforted him. At every gathering of the new Japanese community, Manzo would give a speech. It was noticed that his speech was rather crude but cordial.

Alert to any new venture, Manzo was quick to respond to the Klondike Gold Rush of 1896. The resourceful Manzo is said to have sold picks and pans for the gold miners, resulting in a great profit. With his wealth, he opened three Oriental Art stores in Victoria, registered under the name of J. Manzo Nagano. The "J" was for his adopted name of 'Jack'.

Being such an entrepreneur, Manzo, while busy with his stores, his hotel and while working with the cannery, noticed that the canneries were throwing away some fish that seemed to be of no value at all. Knowing how the Japanese were able to make use of this fish, which he called "hamburger" fish, he salted them in barrels and had them shipped to Japan.

His enterprizing spirit led him to open two restaurants, one in America and another in Yokohama under the name of "Ricksha." However both of them proved failures.

Manzo Nagano was not a religious man, however the story is told about his decision to become a Christian. It was during a special evangelistic campaign that was held in the Japanese community of Victoria led by the Rev. Paul Kanamori, a Salvation Army preacher from Japan. After a very lengthy sermon (Paul Kanamori is noted for his three-hour sermons), when the invitation was given to accept Christ, Manzo rose and made his decision to become a Christian. A humorous aspect of the occasion, was his inappropriate insistence that all his workers accept Christ also.

After the First World War, when Nagano was honored for his war service at a time when Japanese warships were patroling the west coast, his health faded, and he decided to return to Japan, leaving behind two sons to carry on the Nagano name. In 1921, he called his family together, knowing that he would not live too much longer. After this family reunion, Manzo returned to Japan in 1923, back to his village of Kuchinotsu machi, Koraigan, Nagasaki-ken, where he died at the age of 71 on May 1924.

Arichika Ikeda
Discoverer of Ikeda Bay

The following articles were sent by Mrs. Jutaro Tokunaga of Montreal, daughter of Arichika Ikeda, the legendary founder of Ikeda Bay on the Queen Charlottes. The first article was written by her husband, Jutaro Tokunaga who died in 1970 and the second by Izo Arima of Toronto, translated by Mrs. Carey Linde. Both are translations from Japanese and have been published previously in "The Continental Times" *and in* "The Charlottes", *Journal of the Queen Charlotte Islands Museum (Vol. 3, 1973).*

Arichika Ikeda is described in The Charlottes *as "a most unusual man" belonging to a "special breed of adventurers", a man who dominated an exciting period in the history of the Queen Charlottes, "liked and trusted by all he met, no mean feat in those days when racial prejudice . . . was rampant."*

The Exploits of a Pioneer Issei
by Jutaro Tokunaga

A 26-year-old Japanese youth was a passenger aboard the vessel, City of Peking, which left Yokohama for America in December, 1890. The ship was proceeding on the high seas when a Chinese crew member came up to the youth and said: "I found a Japanese boy down below in the cargo section. He is very sick." So the youth went down to see the boy – 15 or 16 years of age – suffering badly from sea sickness. The youth took care of him as best he could.

Arichika Ikeda, age 60

The stowaway told the youth that he wanted very much to go to America but did not have money for the boat fare. The youth begged the captain of the vessel for remission of the boy's illegal action. And when the ship arrived at San Francisco, the captain helped the boy enter the United States. The name of this boy is Shiro Kuroda. He experienced many hardships after entering the United States, yet he studied his way through Military Academy and Boston University.

The writer's main subject, however, is not about Mr. Kuroda but about the youth. His name was Arichika Ikeda and he was the writer's father-in-law.

Mr. Ikeda was born in 1864 in Niigata Province, Japan. A very clever boy, he received an award of honourable mention including a sum of money when fourteen years old from Emperor Meiji at the time of the Emperor's travel to Hokuriku area, and he was deeply affected by this.

When he was sixteen Mr. Ikeda went to Tokyo to study the English language and Chinese Classics, and later to Nagano, Japan, to study at a medical school. But his adventurous spirit and enterprising mind would not keep him at the medical school. He soon journeyed to Karuizawa where he undertook to cultivate virgin land with several farmers who came from his home town. The land belonged to his relative. He planted apple trees and kuri (chestnuts) but these were damaged by rabbits. With seeds imported from America, he also planted tomatoes, cabbage and lettuce. Good soil and a suitable climate aided him in harvesting an abundant vegetable crop. But market for these vegetables were to be found only in Yokohama and Tokyo where the foreign people lived. Transportation costs, however, were too high to make this venture at all economical.

He then tried to raise koi (carp) in the lake inside the property, but failed. Several decades later, Mr. Ikeda revisited this place and felt deep emotion, for it had become a world famous summer resort and the lake in which he had tried to raise koi was named Lake Unjo and became a pleasure centre.

Since his boyhood, Mr. Ikeda had dreamed of doing something in a foreign country. After his arrival in America, the 26-year-old youth worked on a farm in Vacaville, California.

Mr. Ikeda was a Christian and received a title from the head of the church. He taught the message of Christ to the Japanese around Vacaville in the days when gambling was the only pleasure for those people.

Mr. Ikeda organized a labour movement with his comrades in 1893, the first labour union ever organized for the Japanese throughout the Pacific Coast, and he built a meeting place with funds collected from the members. When Mr. Ikeda went to Japan in 1894, he disbanded the Japanese Labour organization and transferred the building to the Christian Church, thus giving the Japanese people in Vacaville their first church building.

Later in the year, he had at his disposal vast properties in Mexico under an arrangement with the Mexican government. With the approval of Buyo Enomoto, then the Minister of Trade and Agriculture of the Japanese government, and Sutemi Chinda, Japanese Consul at San Francisco, he planned to bring Japanese immigrants to Mexico, but this project failed. The following year, Mr. Ikeda returned to America where he rented and worked a farm in California. He did not stay there long, for just at that time the gold rush in the Klondike was taking place.

Accompanied by his friend, Mr. Ohori, adventurous Mr. Ikeda headed for Alaska taking with him cloth, food, equipment (some of which was farm equipment), wheat and vegetable seeds. He invested his entire savings in this trip, expecting to remain in Alaska for some time if it were necessary. His search for gold did not succeed, but he wrote a book about his varied experiences in Alaska. Entitled "Alaska Hyozan Ryoko" (The Journey over the Alaskan Glaciers). The book was published in Tokyo in 1903.

During his two-year stay at Sitka, then capital of Alaska, he studied the various aspects of salmon. Thus, when he returned to Japan in 1902, he was able to negotiate an arrangement with Japanese businessmen to transport salted salmon from Alaska to Japan. The venture proved successful the first year. But in the second year, his schooner, "Higashi Maru" was damaged by fire, resulting in heavy financial loss for Mr. Ikeda.

One day in 1904, he came upon several hundred tons of dead herring cast ashore around Nanaimo, B.C. He struck upon the idea of processing fish oil and manufacturing fish fertilizer. The factory which he built for this venture was unfortunately destroyed by fire. He built another factory, but this time he was forced by the government to shut down the operation because of the wave of anti-Japanese feeling around his area. He then took his case to court and secured a judgment in his favour. This victory was short-lived, because the government then passed a law which stipulated that herring was considered food and should not be made into fertilizer and oil in this particular fishing district of British Columbia.

Undaunted in the face of severe political hindrances, Mr. Ikeda turned to making salted herring, thus opening a vast market in China. He later handed this business over to another Japanese, and it became one of the important Japanese industries in Canada.

With twelve fishermen and a diver, he journeyed north in search of new fishing grounds. They sailed a schooner named Dawson and a gasoline boat named Chisato. The Dawson, designed by Mr. Ikeda, was 150 feet by 33 feet and equipped as a fish packing boat. He came to Moresby Island, one of the Queen Charlotte Islands, where he located in a small bay at the south end. In April, 1906 he discovered copper at Moresby Island. When he journeyed to Victoria to register his copper claim, he could not describe the location by name since it was not given on the map. He drew the shape of the bay on paper and presented it to the government together with a photograph of the bay. A letter he received later from the federal government stated: "This bay shall be named Ikeda Bay forever." It is likely the first time the Canadian map was marked by a Japanese name.

Welcome Arch built for
government officials from
Victoria.
R. Manson, Bowser, Capt Locke,
Dr. H. Young, A. Ikeda

The copper mine was started in 1906. With capital from Japan, a railroad and wharf were built and mining equipment installed. More than seventy workers came from Japan under government permission. At times, workers numbered 150. Mr. Kuroda, who had been helped by Mr. Ikeda to enter the United States 16 years before, came from the east to assist him as his right hand man. The mine was first operated under the name of Awaya, Ikeda and Co. In later years it included Caucasian people, and the name was changed to Ikeda Mines Limited with capitalization of $850,000. It was operated under the supervision of Mr. Ikeda until August, 1920, when it was closed following a drastic drop in the price of copper.

The story about the discovery of the copper mine was published in the papers and magazines along the Pacific coast, and thus encouraged many prospectors to journey to the area. A hotel and bar were built at Jedway, adjacent to Ikeda Bay. The discovery of the mine also caused a sensation in Japan. Books with titles such as "A Great Treasure of the World" and "The Brave Man Arichika Ikeda" were published in that country. The books annoyed Mr. Ikeda because the depictions were much exaggerated.

It was Mr. Ikeda's desire, for many years, to help in the development of the rich natural resources of Canada with Japanese capital. When he returned to Japan in 1919, he negotiated the start of a $25 million company with forty-seven leading financiers of Japan. Named the Canada Kogyo Kabushiki Kaisha (Canadian Industrial Co. Ltd.), the firm had as its aim the purchase of mines and forests in Canada for eventual operation of mines and smelters, paper mills, sawmills and pulp mills. Japanese engineers were dispatched to British Columbia, and their work report was hopeful. But when the company began to put its plan to work, a world-wide depression set in, causing the firm to halt its undertaking.

The fisheries bureau in Japan planned to import live fish over a ten year period in order to improve the quality of fish in Japan. The task of obtaining this fish was given to Mr.

Ikeda. Commencing in 1924 and for many years thereafter, with the co-operation of the U.S. and Canadian Governments, he shipped many millions of rainbow and brook trout eggs each year to the government hatcheries in Japan for propagating them in the rivers and lakes throughout that country. For this work, Mr. Ikeda was awarded recognition at a meeting of the fisheries people in Japan in 1931. It was said then that he had helped greatly in the task of improving fisheries in Japan.

Mr. Ikeda received a patent from the government for a new method of oyster cultivation. He tried his idea at Gambier Island, B.C.

Mr. Ikeda died in Vancouver in 1939 at the age of 75. He was very strong of mind but gentle of hand, and he was a home lover. "One cannot help being poor, nor is it wrong to be rich, but the aim of life is not of these: only to be an honest person." With these last words and holding his son's hand, he slept forever.

Four Years at Ikeda Bay
by Izo Arima

It was July 1913 when Mr. Arichika Ikeda took Mr. Shimizu and me to Ikeda Bay from Vancouver. His house was located in the centre of the Bay, an ideal spot. I could see the tall warehouse for the ore and the mouth of the Bay.

Mr. Ikeda started preparing supper. I watched a few ducks from the window while we were having dinner, and a school of small fish at the mouth of the small brook at the left side of his house. Along this small brook I saw a bird on a tree, the size of a robin with a long beak and colorful tuft on the top of its head. It was trying to catch the fish in the brook. I saw a heron as big as a crane standing on the shore with his long legs, trying to catch the same fish. I saw a huge white bald eagle flying in the sky. Following the eagle was a group of small birds. I asked Mr. Ikeda what was going on. He told me that these birds always go in a group, but once in a while they are attacked by the eagle when they leave the group. Right now the eagle tried to escape from the number of those birds and also the noise.

The sun was still high in the sky when we finished our dinner. He said, "During the summer time, it gets dark around eleven o'clock at night and the dawn is about three in the morning". So Mr. Shimizu and I decided to take out a boat. We started rowing. Mr. Shimizu was quite good as he was a member of the rowing team when he was in school.

Although it was July, I felt a cool breeze and it reminded me of the fall. The bay was surrounded by dense forest and there wasn't a soul around. I knew the mining operation was suspended right now, therefore nobody was around. The quietness was like being in another world. Suddenly Mr. Shimizu started singing as if he was affected by this complete tranquility. His voice echoed in the deep forest.

I slept well that night. The next morning Mr. Ikeda told me to take a turn cooking. He said, "Tomorrow, Shimizu, you get up at six and the following day will be your turn. Both of you take lunch bags with you. Dinner should be cooked by the same person who did the breakfast". Then he explained our job. "The job you are going to do is under the government. According to their plan, this is part of a reclamation. The owner of the mines has to divide the mineral vein into small sections and some of those sections have to be cleared. When you clear that portion of the land you write it down on the form and send the report to the government. Then the government will send you money."

There wasn't any rush, so we did it without haste. On Sundays when the tide was low we went to the mouth of the bay and hunted for some abalone and sea urchins. I saw a small octopus under a small rock, waiting for the crabs or shells to appear. There was a hole with water in front of this octopus house. It is easy to find where an octopus lives as he leaves the empty shells of the crabs he ate. To catch octopus you have to stick your hand under the rock and manage to

Geese at Ikeda Bay

Kotohira Maru, shipwrecked off
Alaska coast, lost in Pacific 40 days,
reached Ikeda Bay Sept 1917, 17 men
including Capt. Haruhiko Shibuya

put your finger between the head and the eyes of the octopus. You can't catch octopus just by pulling its legs. We boiled a small octopus for food. Since then whenever the low tide came we hunted the octopus.

There were some sand beaches to the southeast of Ikeda Bay. During the lowest tide we found that the fish and the crabs were left along the sand beach after the tide went way out. It wasn't a crab hunt but crab picking. We used to take a bucket with us and came back with as much as we could eat. In the lowest tide it fell about thirty feet, which naturally was a real disturbance for the crabs and the small shrimps. However, this situation was a feast to the seagulls and other small birds, and it looked very gay with all the birds on the beach. There were four different kinds of clams along the beach. Food was abundant. The only food we got from Vancouver was rice, miso, soya sauce, sugar and salt.

At Rose Harbour there was a whaling factory and you could get whale meat free. A man called Mr. Shimabukuro who worked for the whaling plant came to work with us as he didn't have much to do at the plant. Also Mr. Kyosaku Yoshida who was brought up in the same area of Japan as Mr. Ikeda came to work with us. With that additional labour our work went very fast.

One day while we were working I felt cold and had a headache. In spite of Mr. Ikeda's treatment my temperature rose steadily and I lost consciousness. After a week I started having some appetite and ate loosely cooked rice, toast and soup. When I recovered completely Mr. Ikeda told me that at one point he thought I wouldn't make it through. Mr. Ikeda once wanted to become a doctor so he had some knowledge of medicine. He also kept quite a supply of medicine at hand.

Our work ended in September. Most of us went back to Vancouver. I saw movies, went to Stanley Park and visited friends. One day Mr. Ikeda took me to a Chinese dinner. As I hadn't had Chinese food for a long time I over-ate. That night I was attacked by a severe pain. My stomach was as hard as a rock. After being examined by three doctors, it was diagnosed as appendicitis. I stayed in hospital over three weeks and it cost more than 300 dollars. Mr. Ikeda paid it completely.

In November only Mr. Ikeda and I were back at Ikeda Bay. One day Mr. Ikeda asked me to learn how to use guns. He had three different kinds of rifles and allowed me to freely use any of them. Between November and February was the deer season and I was told to go to Jedway to get a licence from the police. Ordinarily a licence cost $2 and a prospect exploration licence cost $8 for a year. I got the latter one and thought that we would never get hungry again. As soon as I got home from Jedway, I sewed the badge onto my hat. I carried the small rifle on my shoulder and walked around the house humming to myself. Mr. Ikeda said, "You look just like a little boy, and as if thousands of buds suddenly opened up in you. I can't stop smiling this year as I have you around. I have been all alone before."

Suddenly I saw a small bird land on the very top of the roof. Why don't you shoot. It's a grouse," said Mr. Ikeda. I aimed at the bird. I had never shot a bird before and I felt sorry for it. I even shivered a bit. "Shoot it right now," said Mr. Ikeda who was standing next to me. I missed the bird. Mr. Ikeda encouraged me to try again and he added that the bird wouldn't fly away until you shot it down. My second trial was a success. We cooked it for supper that night. The meat was tender and the taste was good.

In November there were many ducks around Ikeda Bay. I could count about ten different coloured ducks, the mallard duck, donkey duck, white duck, diver duck, etc. They were all swimming around in a group. In November many dead salmon were floating in the river after spawning. Many ducks came to eat those dead fish. Each bird – ducks, crows, eagles – made different noises and it sounded very lively. Ducks had rather extravagent tastes as they ate only the eyes of the fish.

Once Mr. Ikeda took me to the mouth of the river and taught me how to use the shotgun. I shot one duck with a blue neck which was delicious. But this particular kind of duck was hard to shoot. They often stay in the shallows and stick their heads in the water and their tails above the surface. I found that the best time of the day to shoot these blue-necked ducks was early in the morning when the tide was coming in. I hid myself in the bush. During that season I went there every morning to shoot. In October the salmon started running up the river for spawning which brought many ducks to eat the eggs.

After devoting my days to hunting, Christmas came. On Christmas morning Mr. Ikeda asked, "Would you take some gifts to the people in Jedway." He handed me three different parcels. I started climbing up the steep hill to cross the mountain, carrying the big bag on my shoulder. In spite of the usual December weather, Christmas day turned out to be beautiful. The sun was bright. The path on the mountain was very steep. I climbed up step by step, gasping. When I reached the top I was sweating. I sat on a stone and took a big breath. When I gazed in front of me there was nothing but the continuation of dense forest. There was no wind, no birds, no bears. Absolute silence. I thought that this stillness was the very one which was said to be the death of all the creatures. I wondered if there existed any other place with such stillness in the world.

Jedway is at the bottom of the hill. It was just like Ikeda Bay as the mine operation was closed. I stopped at Thompson's first. He was the caretaker of the mine and they knew me as they had visited Ikeda Bay a few times. As soon as Mrs. Thompson saw me at the door she ran towards me, saying, "My boy," and she embraced me with her arms which were just the same size as my thigh. I thought I was going to suffocate. She weighed more than 200 lbs. and I had never been embraced by a woman that size. She was in jolly spirits and she said, "Please come in. Please sit down," putting her hand on my shoulder. She brought Christmas cakes and some fruit. She was so happy that she kept touching my cheeks and hair. I felt I was treated like a little boy but I thought that was because they didn't have any children. Her husband kept smiling. I left a Christmas gift for them.

The next house I visited was Prescott who was the

police officer. They were also delighted with my visit. Mrs. Prescott ran into the kitchen and brought me some food. She said, "This is a home-made abalone pie, and home-made wild berry wine." The pie and the wine were delicious. When my face became red Mrs. Prescott laughed and said, "You got drunk."

The last house I visited was MacFee who owned the hotel. She was a widow of 34 or 35. She didn't have any children either. She was a very good looking lady. She was also very delighted to see me. Since there wasn't anybody staying at the hotel, she took me to the dining room. She said, "It's almost lunch time." And she cooked fried eggs for me. She talked as if her lover was visiting her and her conversation didn't seem to stop. I wanted to listen to this beautiful woman's story but I noticed the time. I excused myself as it was getting dark, and I handed a gift to her. She said, "I got some freshly baked bread for you to take." I stepped outside and thought they were so excited by my visit because of the isolation and their not having children or not seeing people.

When I returned home Mr. Ikeda said, "Thank you for all the trouble. You must have charmed them with your fine character and they must have been very happy to see you. I am cooking Christmas dinner. We will have duck instead of a turkey." It was a good Christmas dinner.

New Year's Day came. Mr. Ikeda said, "We don't have either sake or mochi to celebrate. Let's make some poems instead." My poem made more or less by Mr. Ikeda turned out like this.

> I made up my mind to put all my effort
>   into my work
> To see the sun rise on the New Year's morning
> My heart is full of emotion
> Looking at the sky where I was born
> I pray with my head bowed

Towards the end of the New Year's holiday Mr. Ikeda said, "I have some business in Vancouver. I am afraid I have to leave you alone here, so I've asked Mr. Hirami who works at Mr. Mukai's camp to come and stay with you." Mr. Hirami was brought up in Kishu in Japan. Mr. Ikeda also said, "You might have some visitors while I am away, particularly as it's winter time now. You can feed them, as we have plenty of food, but let them cut some wood for us. You will be the boss during my absence." After Mr. Ikeda left Mr. Hirami arrived. We took turns every morning hunting ducks for our meals.

As Mr. Hirami was brought up in a fishing village, he knew all about fishing. One morning he said, "Let's go fishing today as it is a nice day." He had already prepared his fishing rod and salted herring for the bait. "First, let's find the right spot to fish. It's not true that the fish are everywhere in the ocean," he said. We rowed further out. Mr. Hirami put the fishing line in the water and checked if there were any fish. "I caught one," he said. It was a red snapper called amadai in Japan. He tried again and caught four more in a few minutes. When we got back to the house Mr. Hirami cooked some fish and he also cut some to eat raw. I cooked some rice. It was a superb dinner. We could hardly move after dinner as we ate so much.

Just off Jedway there was a fish plant owned by Mr. Mukai. The plant was closed during the months of January to April until the herring season. During that period no unemployment insurance existed; therefore during the winter those who worked at the plant used to come to our mine. As I was substituting for Mr. Ikeda while he was away I told them that they could stay for free if they cut wood for us. They were willing to take that job. One of them, Mr. Kawada, was good at making noodles. Mr. Hirami continued hunting ducks. A man called Mr. Kaminaka who had a gasoline boat lived in Jedway. He often used his boat as transportation for the government officials, surveyors, explorers or mining engineers. He received some money doing that job. He also was given a mine at Rose Harbour from some white man who thought there wasn't any future for the mine. Mr. Kaminaka held that mine for over ten

Mine entrance

Arichika Ikeda - right

Mrs. Archie Ikeda, Mr. T. Shimoisaka
Mr. Archie Ikeda, Capt. Shibuya
baby Arimoto

years and he sold it for $35,000. Using that sum of money as capital he hired some Japanese and shipped salted herring to Japan. He made a fortune out of that business and then he did some lumber business. He shipped the lumber to Japan and was a great success.

A man called Mr. Fujihira who used to be a cook at the mining camp baked delicious bread. He said to bake cake you must put your hand in the oven then start counting from one to twenty-five. When you get to twenty-five if you find its too hot to keep your hand in the oven, then you put the cake dough in. I learned a great deal from him.

After the men left for Mukai's fish plant I was left all alone. In the daytime I cut wood and when the weather was good I dug some soil to make a vegetable garden. I got a lot of rest and read some magazines Mr. Ikeda sent. It was so quiet. I had a white cat called Tom who always stayed with me even when I was taking a bath.

One night when I was reading a book in the parlor, I heard a loud noise. I immediately thought that it could be a bear. I felt rather uneasy and went to bed immediately. In the end I became just like a bird which stays up only during the daylight. This habit naturally improved my health. My mind became very peaceful and as if I were a superhuman being.

Once in two weeks the big boat came in the bay. What a joy to hear the horn. The mail and food were unloaded on the wharf. People from the radio station were there. A man called Mr. Heino who was Finnish and owned the mine at Copper Island just out of Ikeda Bay came with his big gasoline boat. Ever since he discovered the copper mine in the little island, he had lived there for twenty-five years with only a dog as a companion.

It was like a festival for us when the boat arrived. We talked to each other at the wharf. Although Mr. Heino got only matches and powdered milk in each shipment, he had the healthiest looking skin and body. Every October Mr. Heino used to ask Mr. Ikeda to look after his dog when he sailed down to Vancouver with his gasoline boat changing into a sail boat for the trip. It took him days to get down to Vancouver. On his way back he shot deer on the coast of the mainland and brought one deer for Mr. Ikeda.

A man called Mr. Smith lived in Jedway who couldn't read or write but he understood things well. He often came to Ikeda Bay on his little boat to sell vegetables. Mr. Campbell who was nearly 70 lived in his neighbourhood and kept saying, "Some day soon I will marry a Japanese girl." I was very amazed that each one of them were like superhuman beings.

In April Mr. Ikeda came back from Vancouver. "It's time for the garden. We have four acres of land. Just one acre will be plenty. We seeded spinach, carrots and others and planted cabbages and potatoes. I noticed that many different kinds of berry flowers started blooming which attracted many humming birds. There were two kinds of humming birds. One was red and the other was light green. On a sunny day the sky was covered with them. The red humming bird had a tendency to fly down from high up in the sky with amazing speed and a squeaking noise. It was a very pretty bird and I shot them with my specially made bullet and sent the birds to my friends.

It was getting very cheerful outside with a variety of birds singing. One of the birds sounded as if it said, "Japanese, shinè, shinè (die, die)." The bird first said "Japanese" twice very slowly and then raised up its voice and said "shinè" three times. When I lived near Burnaby Lake in B.C. later on, I heard the same sound from the same bird. I once told a man who was with me, "Listen, it says, Japanese." He was a white man, by the way, and he said to me sourly, "It says, Canadian." The bird at Burnaby Lake didn't say it as clear as the one in Ikeda Bay. In any event, that was a very unpleasant bird saying Japanese die, die.

I heard the grouse in the woods like beating drums. Since the sound echoed through the mountain, it was very hard to locate the bird. From early May many flies appeared and bit our faces and hands. They disappeared by July. Mosquitoes appeared at night but they didn't bother us as we had mosquito nets. They disappeared by September. Salmon berries started ripening in June and as they became riper the bears came to eat.

One day as I walked along the mine I came across a big bear. Since both sides of the wooded road were thick with berry bushes I couldn't avoid the bear so we met each other face to face. For awhile the bear didn't notice my approach for he was concentrating on eating berries. I had a shotgun with only one barrel so I thought I would rather not shoot the bear in case I missed him. I stamped on a board very hard in order to make the bear realize my presence. The bear looked at me and suddenly turned around and started walking in front of me. I followed the bear. After walking about a block and a half there was a bridge. At the end of the bridge the berry bushes ended and one side of the road opened up into a hill. The bear didn't seem to go into the bush. Preparing for the worst I aimed at the bear's face with my gun and I shouted as loud as I could, which scared the bear and it ran up the mountain.

I came across bears many times in the mountain but in most cases as soon as the bears noticed my appearance, they entered the bush and found a big rock or big stump of a tree and stared at me for a few minutes. I stared back. Most of them opened and closed their eyes many times before they took off. I have never seen the bear which walked in front of me.

One day Mr. Kawada came with his little boat and asked, "Mr. Ikeda, I found something glittering in this stone on the beach when I was resting from the fishing. I brought it with me in case it was gold. Would you take a look?" It was pure gold in the stone, the size of a green pea. Mr. Kawada told us that he saw many such stones but it was the only one which had something so shiny. Mr. Kawada used to work in a gold mine in Japan and he saw the same type of stone there. Mr. Kawada often brought us salted abalone. He was the so-called general manager of Mukai's camp. He told me that Mr. Mukai introduced him to a Japanese lady and he said that they were going to get married. He received a letter from her but he could neither read nor write. He asked me to read her letter and write her a reply. When I did him this favour he was very happy.

One sunny and calm day Mr. Ikeda said, "Let's go fishing today and also get some sea chickens. Bring along your gun." We rowed the boat off Ikeda Bay. When we reached the spot with small rocky islands we saw many sea chickens flying between the islands. They looked just like chickens. I shot two from the boat. At the same time I saw a seagull on the island. I climbed up and found its nest. The nest was made very neatly with dry grass and twigs and there were two eggs the same size as duck eggs. I took one only as I felt sorry. The seagull didn't fly away but watched me. I was very amazed that the bird was so quiet.

Mr. Ikeda kept several chickens around his house without a fence. They could feed themselves easily on the beach or bushes, and they laid many eggs. One morning when I was feeding them I noticed a different shape of bird eating with the chickens. I looked carefully and noticed that it was a grouse. I took the gun and shot it. I saw many times the grouse with their babies. I couldn't shoot them when they were together as I felt very emotional.

The assessment work started that year like the previous year. Once I went to Rose district to work. It was located on the left side of the mountain in the centre of Ikeda Bay. I was very surprised at the sight of that small mountain, looking all rusted with iron. Mr. Ikeda said, "There is plenty of iron in Canada but they can't make much profit out of it, as the labour cost is too high. In the Queen Charlottes iron is everywhere. When the time comes if the price of iron goes up they will dig it up."

At the bottom of the mountain we saw a huge cave, 12 feet by 12 feet. It was large enough for people to live in. I thought that once some Indians lived there. Beside the cave a small creek was running. It must have been an ideal place to live. In the same area we saw an old cedar tree and about 4 feet by 4 feet of the bark was pulled off. I thought that an Indian must have taken it off to make rugs and baskets. I was

36

told that a long time ago the whole Queen Charlotte Islands was inhabited by Indians but some infection destroyed almost all the population.

Two young English radio operators came to the station in Ikeda Bay. The one called Mr. Hassell, who used to be a soldier, visited us very often. He was good at shooting the ducks in the air. I visited him once as he said he was bored. On the top of his front door I saw a human skull. He said, "Don't you think it's a fine piece. I found it in the back of the mountain. It's an Indian's skull." Then he put boxing gloves in my hands. I tried very hard to hit him, but my every attempt was in vain. After the game we had a cup of tea with some bread and jam.

One evening after supper we heard the chickens running around the house clucking. We rushed outside. A huge eagle was attacking. One cock was brave enough to attack the eagle back. The cock didn't seem to have a chance. As soon as the eagle noticed us it flew up to the top of the tree, and looked down. It was too high for us to shoot. Mr. Ikeda was looking at the eagle and said, "With my rifle I will get that bird. I once used to be a senior officer in the army. You will see my skill." He shot. We cooked that eagle and it tasted delicious, red like beef and there wasn't any smell. I thought maybe it was because the eagle ate nothing but fresh meat.

A whaler entered into Ikeda Bay to get some rest. At the bow of the vessel the cannon was attached and the harpoon was inserted in the tip of the cannon. To the harpoon the thick rope was attached. When the whale was caught the rope was wound up by the winch. The sailor on the whaler brought us the meat of porpoise and we found that porpoise steak was delicious and tasted like beef. Mr. Iwasaki, the engineer of the whaler, shot a small bear while he was in the bay. We cooked and ate it but the meat wasn't too good and had some sort of smell.

At the end of August a great number of salmon came into the bay. During mealtimes we enjoyed watching the salmon leaping on the surface of the sea. It became my job after dinner to set the net which we borrowed from Mr.

Mukai. Two kinds of salmon came up to Ikeda Bay. One was called coho and the other was dog salmon. Salmon were very clever fish. It was almost impossible to catch them in the net in the daytime but it was even harder in the evening. I often found that most of the fish in the net were eaten by seals and they only left the head and bones. If there was plenty for the seals to eat in the net they only ate the best part of the fish which was around the head and left the rest of the fish for me. Besides eating the fish they broke the net and kept me busy mending all the time.

The dog fish were hard to take out as they tangled themselves in the net. The sharks cut the net in many places which also kept me busy mending. As the salmon started to run in the river many seals followed them. The mouth of each river was covered with bald-headed eagles. When female salmon started laying eggs the male salmon built some beds with small gravel and sand using their noses and then smoothed it with their tails. I thought it was a very clever thing to do. Many ducks came to eat those eggs. After laying eggs the dog salmon became black and died but coho changed into red and it seemed they returned into the sea as I didn't see any dead coho in the river.

In July, 1914 World War I broke out. That incident brought the price of copper up again. The Ikeda Mine was reopened. We started our operation on a smaller scale. We called the people who used to work in the mine from all over B.C. One of them was Mr. Denji Takano. He was about my age and we were the youngest of them all. Mr. Ikeda said, "You two are going to take jobs as miners." Every morning the ore and the disposable stones were taken out. The ore was dumped out on the bank and the waste stones went to the valley. It was a hard job, and the place had to be emptied for the night shift crew.

One day when we were doing the job in the mine, Mr. Ikeda came and said, "Do you think that you can take all that ore out by 6 o'clock?" We worked like crazy that day and we finished at 5:30 and we went home very proudly. Mr. Ikeda came back and said, "Did you really finish the job?" Mr.

Takano said, "We took 18 carsfull of load out." "That means 18 tons. That's excellent," said Mr. Ikeda. As a matter of fact Mr. Ikeda was very pleased with the result of our work.

As the mine operation progressed many geologists came. For those who were whites we had to prepare western meals. I became a cook. Not only that but I was in charge of taking care of the garden, fishing, etc.

One Sunday morning some of us decided to go to the hot spring island about twenty-five miles away from Ikeda Bay. We got there in only two hours. We noticed the colour of the vegetation of the island was much darker than anywhere else in the island because of the warm earth. As we climbed to the top of the mountain the hot water was running into the small pond which was too hot to go in. A little further down below there was another pond but it was still too hot. We found a third one which was the right temperature. We all soaked in that pond. The water was so clear that we could see through to our toes.

Reopening the Ikeda Mine brought many official guests. To entertain them Mr. Ikeda always kept good whiskey and ordered a barrel of Japanese sake from Japan to encourage those who worked at the mine. Mr. Prescott, the police officer at Jedway, liked sake and he often came to join us to drink. One day Mr. Prescott left our place after having some drinks. It was about six o'clock when he left. Mr. Ikeda used his handmade telephone to inform Mrs. Prescott about his departure. The telephone was placed in the box with six regular batteries and connected by ordinary wire through trees to Jedway.

Soon after he left the typical black clouds on this island covered the sky and it became a bad storm with strong wind and rain. About a quarter past seven we received a call from Mrs. Prescott that her husband had not come home yet. We thought he should have been home by seven. Mr. Ikeda phoned her back around seven thirty but he wasn't home yet either. Something must have happened on his way home. Mr. Ikeda said, "Izo, we have to go and search for him at once." We put rain coats on and had lanterns with each of us. We started tracing the way which Mr. Prescott went. We kept yelling. The storm was getting worse. When we neared the top of the mountain the narrow path changed into a brook, and suddenly from the bottom of the hill we heard somebody saying "Hello" to us. We saw Mr. Prescott climbing up the cliff, soaking wet. We pulled him up from the cliff. He told us that he lost his steps and fell down into the bottom of the valley and he was unconscious there for a while until he heard us yelling. He saw the light of our lamps which urged him to climb up the hill like crazy. We were so happy to see him safe. We took him to his home. Mrs. Prescott received him with tears. We returned to our home very late that night.

My second New Year's day at Ikeda Bay arrived. They were prosperous days for Ikeda Bay. On New Year's we received many people from other camps. To celebrate we started drinking sake. As we got drunker some started singing songs. Mr. Ikeda then said, "Izo, you have been drinking since the beginning yet you look like you haven't touched a thing. I have never seen someone like you. I think you better stay away from drinking." I quit drinking from then.

One day in the middle of January, the wind was too strong even for ducks who kept themselves deep in the valley. I shot blue necked ducks that day. In early February we had an unexpected snowfall. That morning on my way to the wharf I saw geese honking and flying around. After my work I came back with a rifle. All nine of them were still on the beach with one goose keeping watch for the enemy's approach. I aimed at the nearest one. It seemed to me that all of them took off. Next morning I went back to the beach to see if I had been lucky enough to shoot one. I counted the geese and noticed that one was missing. I found one dead on the beach but the meat of the bird had already gone. I thought that the eagle must have eaten it. I was told that the goose is a very affectionate bird and if one of them is killed, the rest would stay in the place instead of taking off. I decided to come back to the same spot next day. It was still snowing the next day and the bushes looked as if hundreds of flowers were blooming. I saw the same number of geese on the other side of the shore eating something, but they were taking turns watching for the enemy. I kept myself very low. The tide was up at that time which put me in a better position for shooting. I successfully shot one. The rest of them were flying around the dead one and flew to the nearby cemetery where two Japanese employees who died by the dynamite accident in the Ikeda Mine were buried. I hid the one I shot in the bush so that it wouldn't be eaten by the eagle, and I tried for another goose. It was a success again and I went home with two huge geese the size of turkeys on my shoulder. One of them we sent to the camp. Later on somebody from the camp shot five of them and I shot the last one. After that there weren't any geese left.

In early April when I was at Mr. Ikeda's office located by the beach, Mr. Ikeda said, "Izo, a huge goose is sitting on the other side of the beach. Why don't you shoot it?" I wondered why one goose was left alone as all the rest of the geese had already migrated. I shot that goose. Since I had a prospector licence, I could shoot any time and also I always carried guns as my hobby.

July and August were the best months in the year on the islands. It wasn't too hot or too cold. One day Mr. Ikeda said, "I have a place I wanted to check for a long time. Why don't you come with me." We took our gasoline boat and started our exploration. A little southwest of Ikeda Bay was a fairly big island called Burnaby. To make a short cut, instead of going around Burnaby Bay, we had to go through the channel. We knew there was a very shallow spot in the channel, and in order to make it through we had to go at high tide. Mr. Ikeda looked at his watch and said, "We have plenty of time to go through." He navigated the boat by himself, but he was wrong. When we went about half way through the channel the boat was aground. We couldn't move for the next five hours. As we watched the tide, it went away quickly and our boat ended up on the hill. Hundreds of crabs were crawling around and there were abalone and sea urchins too.

Inside the sea urchin was meat the shape of a half moon. You ate the raw meat and it was very tasty. The native Indians call them sea eggs and said that you got very strong if you ate them.

We saw some rock oysters in the hollow of the rock. I was told that they never moved from the spot. You could use the empty shell as a little dish as it had a very lovely colour inside. Once you taste rock oyster, you never forget its taste. There was abundant food around as there wasn't anybody living there. We took a bucketful of shells. Around five in the evening the tide came back and the boat started floating at last. After an hour's sail toward the mainland (Moresby), we took a left turn and went into a small bay. The bay was extremely quiet and surrounded by mountains. We saw a bear at the mouth of the bay watching us very curiously as if he had never seen a man before. We landed and made a campfire and had our supper. We slept in the boat that night and got up early in the morning to start our exploration.

We took the trail along the river which ran out in the centre of the bay. At the mouth of the river there were several stakes driven in. They looked very dark and thin as they had stayed in the water so long. Those stakes were driven by the Indians a long time ago in order to catch salmon. When the fish went up into the river during the high tide they threw branches above the stakes in the river and after the tide had gone, they caught those which were trapped among the branches. As we walked further up we came to a very narrow but fine path. "Mr. Ikeda, is there anybody living in such places?" I said. "It's a good road. It's a road for the bear," said Mr. Ikeda. "The bear can make a nice road as they walk with their four legs," said Mr. Ikeda and he laughed. Soon after that the nice path disappeared. I said to Mr. Ikeda, "The path has disappeared." Mr. Ikeda replied that the bear is clever enough not to let anybody follow to where they live. We came to a huge meadow. The wind was gently blowing and a horsefly landed on my shoulder. Some frogs were jumping around us. I had never seen either of them at Ikeda Bay. Mr. Ikeda said, "This is the narrowest point in the island and closer to the Pacific Ocean which makes the temperature milder than at Ikeda Bay. We started walking toward the west until we saw the white rocky mountain. Mr. Ikeda hit the surface of the rock with his prospector pick and said, "Now I am quite satisfied. I would like to go to the west coast but will wait till next time." We left the spot and returned to the boat and left the next morning.

In my fourth summer at Ikeda Bay I met a doctor who came with the Japanese life insurance agent from Vancouver. To make a special treat for them I took them to catch mountain trout at the biggest river in the bay. I threw the lighted dynamite in the river where the fish were making a swirl. Naturally I caught a basketful of fish. They told us that they had never seen such a way of fishing before. They enjoyed the fish very much.

In August of that year, Mr. Ikeda said, "Izo, you worked very hard. Your mother and I studied Chinese together and you seem to me like my own son. I want to make you a success and for that I want you to improve your English more in Vancouver." I decided to go to Vancouver and left Ikeda Bay full of memories.

P.S.: Several years ago my son was sent to the Queen Charlottes from Ottawa to investigate the Indians on the island. He did not stop at Ikeda Bay but he said that about a hundred people were working at Jedway and the Japanese boat was loading iron ore. The cars were running in the village of Skidegate and he stayed in the hotel there. The population in the whole island is about 5,000.

Lion Island

L to R: Work shop for boat building and repair;
(tsukemono) pickle and vegetable storage; farm
tool shed; bunk house upstairs and warehouse downstairs; community hall and dining
room; Oikawa family residence.

Memorial Service for Jinzaburo Oikawa

Jinzaburo Oikawa
Adventurer

*One day a couple by the name of Mr. and Mrs. Tom Oikawa of
Richmond, B.C. visited me. I had married them at New Denver,
during the Second World War and, renewing old acquaintances
we talked about my project of writing about the lives of a few
Japanese Canadian pioneers. In the course of our conversation,
I discovered that Tom's relative, Mr. Jinzaburo Oikawa, was
famed for trying to establish a Japanese colony in Canada. So
here is the unusual story.*

Jinzaburo Oikawa, born in 1853, in Masubuchi, Yonekawa-
mura, Tome-gun, Miyagi-ken, Japan, was a successful
farmer and owner of a silk factory. One day Jinzaburo's
friend received an unusually wonderful letter from Mr.
Soemon Sato, who had immigrated to Canada, telling about
the abundance of salmon in the Fraser River and the practice
of discarding the dog salmon and fish roe into the river. So in
1896, Jinzaburo came to Vancouver to find out whether the
story in the letter was true or not.

Jinzaburo was 43 years old. He and his wife, Uino, had
two sons, Taijiro age 18, and Michie 10. He got a passport as
a businessman and came to Canada as a second class
passenger aboard an American ship. It took about 20 days to
cross the Pacific Ocean in those days. On board the ship he
met a Japanese Methodist minister, Rev. Goro Kaburagi,
the first Japanese Methodist minister and founder of the
Japanese Methodist Church in Canada. Jinzaburo asked the
minister about Canada and Rev. Kaburagi told him many
things. He also taught him English so Oikawa could at least
sign his name and speak a little English.

While waiting for Mr. Soemon Sato, Mr. Oikawa spent
a few days in a Japanese hotel on Powell Street in Vancouver. However, Soemon did not come. As Jinzaburo
Oikawa could not speak English, Rev. Kaburagi got him an
interpreter, Mr. Masutaro Miyagawa, and together with his
interpreter Jinzaburo went by horse and buggy to Steveston.

45

He was surprised that the Fraser River was so big but was disappointed because he could not see the big salmon as the river was not clear like rivers of Japan. Next they visited a fishing cannery where he saw fish roe being tossed into the river. Then later they visited Mr. and Mrs. Koemon Nakabayashi whom Jinzaburo had met briefly in a hotel at Yokohama, Japan. Through Mr. Nakabayashi's advice Jinzaburo actually started fishing that following summer and during the 'off fishing' season, he worked at a sawmill. Later working at a logging camp, he earned $1.50 a day while a white logger got $5. Oikawa left the logging camp and came to Vancouver to see Rev. Kaburagi who asked him what he discovered after working for one year. Jinzaburo replied that in order to succeed, a group of people with the same ideal and understanding must help each other and work together; and these people could only be found among relatives and friends of the same village. However, Rev. Kaburagi had another thought; that through assimilation Japanese Canadians could raise their standard of living to that of the white Canadians and thus have the same opportunities as all Canadians.

Jinzaburo went back to Steveston and while wondering what to do next the long awaited visit of Soemon Sato came. How happy they were to meet; talking all night they discussed the ways and means of building their own fishing village. The next day they walked the shores of the Fraser River from Steveston eastward as far as Sunbury a distance of 17 kilometers where there were a fishing cannery and a few fishermen's houses. They thought this an ideal place to start a settlement. The first thing they needed was a place to build houses. Fortunately they located the owner of a big tract of land along the west bank of the river which had a cotton tree forest. Soemon and Jinzaburo contracted to cut down the trees for $75 an acre, and at the same time obtained the lease to the land and the right to build houses there. Through the owner of the land, they contracted to fish for salmon for the cannery. They built three log houses and bought three fishing boats and the cannery also rented two boats to them. There were eight men from Miyagi-ken,

Japan, but unfortunately they were not fishermen, and half of them could not even swim. Teaching them how to handle the boats and cast nets was not easy. However, they did learn, became accustomed to the water and later became professional fishermen.

After they built three log houses, Mr. Oikawa started the salted dog salmon and salted salmon roe business. He secured the market among Japanese who were working on the railway and logging camps. Soon twenty men lived in the three log houses and worked together. Jinzaburo wanted to expand the business by bringing in more Japanese from his native village in Japan. At that time the farmers in his village were deep in the post-war depression and had also suffered two years of famine.

He left Canada in December of 1898 and arrived home in Japan on January 1899. He tried very hard to get immigrants to Canada from among his relatives and villagers but because many found it difficult to raise the $60 per person transportation fee and also because of the uncertainty of the future, only nine people came as immigrants to Canada in May 1899. These included four of his friends and four members of his household, his wife Uino, sons Taijiro and Michie, and Uino's maid Yaeno and Jinzaburo himself.

When they arrived in Sunbury, they found their log houses ready for them. The communal life meant everyone ate together and Uino had to work hard to feed 30 people with the help of Yaeno. Unfortunately it was too much for Uino and she became ill. She had a heart condition before she came to Canada. On the one hand Jinzaburo Oikawa's business prospered, but his wife's health worsened and she was sent to the New Westminster hospital for 10 days. After she was discharged from the hospital her condition did not improve and she realized that her days were numbered and so asked young Yaeno to take her place by marrying Jinzaburo after she died. Uino's fervent wish was to return to Japan and escorted by her son, Taijiro, she left Canada in October, 1900 and she passed away one and a half months after they arrived in Japan.

Out in Sunbury, the Oikawa colony were having many problems. The white fishermen in Steveston went on strike, but the Japanese would not. The trouble extended to Sunbury and Lion Island areas.

The death of Uino caused great confusion in the colony. Finally Jinzaburo and Yaeno married and the Oikawa colony moved to Lion Island. Later Don Island was added to the settlement. These islands were commonly called Oikawa Shima (Oikawa Island) among the Japanese. Yaeno found difficulty as the only woman among thirty men. Fortunately Masutaro Miyagawa brought a couple to the Island, the Nishiyamas, who helped her greatly. More land was cleared and houses built and also a factory to process salted dog salmon. Ten more villagers from Japan arrived including three women. In 1902, after one and a half years of marriage a healthy son, Eiji, was born to Jinzaburo and Yaeno.

In 1903, Jinzaburo returned to Japan to bring more people from his native village and also to establish a company at Yokohama which would handle his products, the salted dog salmon and salmon roe. Unfortunately the villagers were not ready for his plan so Jinzaburo, after staying in Japan for three months, returned to Canada to find the kitchen house with its dining rooms destroyed by fire and the colony ready to split into two groups — one group to remain with the Oikawas and the other to go to Don Island with Soeman Sato. Finally, 15 people left with Soeman and they were given five fishing boats.

The same year Oikawa called a carpenter, a welder, and a machinist from Japan, paying for their fares, and five others came who paid for their own way. In 1904, their first daughter, Shima, was born and his son, Michie, age 19, who was studying in Japan, came home. Jinzaburo was surprised at Michie's knowledge and good manners.

The Russo-Japanese War ended after the great sea battle on May 27 and 28, 1905, and the people of Japan were suffering a grave economic depression when Jinzaburo decided to go back to Japan again to bring more Japanese to Canada. He had been introduced to Mr. Saburo Yoshie, a clerk at the Japanese Consulate in Vancouver by Rev. Kaburagi and Yoshie and Oikawa became fast friends. They talked about the labour shortage in Canada due to the construction of the C.P.R. and Jinzaburo spoke of his plan to bring more Japanese immigrants to his settlement.

On April, 1906, Jinzaburo Oikawa again reached his native village and immediately began to persuade his relatives to go to Canada in order to save the village from starvation. As it was very difficult to enter Canada now as an immigrant, his plan was to have the villagers enter Canada illegally — they were to enter Canada as ship-wrecked ocean going fishermen. And, on August 31, 1906 the Suian Maru, a 200-ton sailing boat, with Captain Nishikiori at the helm, set sail for Canada with 80 men and three women.

Not one of the voyagers, except Mr. Oikawa, had ever crossed the Pacific Ocean before. They sailed for 50 long and difficult days; Jinzaburo had to face not only the rough seas but also the many complaints of the passengers. Finally, they neared Beacher Bay, Vancouver Island, B.C. Although they knew that their journey had not ended — their destination being Lion Island — they were relieved to be in sight of Canadian soil. The plan was for one group to travel to the Island by land and the other by water. Unfortunately they landed near the naval base at Esquimalt and were arrested by the Canadian Navy. At normal times, these people would have been deported to Japan, but at that time Canada needed huge numbers of cheap labour for the construction of the C.P.R. This group from Miyagi-ken were admitted as immigrants.

Jinzaburo Oikawa returned to Japan in 1917 and with the loss of the leader, the Oikawa settlement did not survive. Although there are several reasons given why he returned to Japan, the main reason was the loss of his beloved son, Eiji, aged 10, in a drowning accident in the Fraser River.

After he went back to his native Yonekawa-mura, he engineered the drainage of a shallow lake enabling the villagers to farm the new tract of land.

This colourful man died on April 4, 1929.

Jiro Inouye, Pioneer Farmer and Yasutaro Yamaga, Founder of Nipponia Home

When you consider the stories of Japanese Canadian pioneers, the importance that agriculture played in their lives should not be forgotten. Among many notable pioneers in this field were two outstanding leaders, Jiro Inouye and Yasutaro Yamaga. It was while I was working for Jiro Inouye on his strawberry farm at Trunk Road, Port Haney, B.C., from 1922 to 1923 that I met Yasutaro Yamaga.

Jiro Inouye, a son of a samurai, was born in Saga-ken, Japan in 1870. He received his early education at his native village and later studied law at Waseda University in Tokyo, one of the best educational institutions in Japan. Right after the China-Japan war (1894-1895), he went to Taiwan and worked for a wholesale food business. After a few years, he returned to Japan and engaged in several different occupations. In 1897, he went to Belgium to learn the glass manufacturing business but as this enteprise was not successful, he went to Seattle, Washington, U.S.A. where he became an adviser to Masajiro Furuya, the most successful Japanese merchant of that time.

Jiro did not stay there very long as he wanted to help Japanese immigrants so he came to Canada and in 1906 bought 20 acres of land in Haney and started to grow strawberries. He found it profitable and wrote many articles in the Japanese newspapers, urging people to start farming. When anti-Japanese sentiments in B.C. became intense, many Japanese fishermen had their licences taken away by the government and so were without work. Many sawmill workers also began to worry about their families' futures. A number of these people followed Jiro Inouye's advice and moved into the Fraser Valley to try their hand at farming. Needing strawberry pickers, Inouye advertised and like many other Japanese, I answered the advertisement, was hired and worked from the summer of 1922. During the winter I attended McLean High School in Maple Ridge and taught Japanese language to the Japanese Canadian farmers' children. This was how I came to know Inouye.

Jiro Inouye was a man of vision and an idealist. He taught his followers that by living peacefully, side by side with their white neighbours, by sharing in the educational needs of their children, by paying their taxes and by acting as good citizens the Japanese Canadians could be integrated into the Canadian mainstream. And, because the anti-Japanese movement was increasing in B.C., he urged Japanese Canadian farmers in Haney not to offend their white neighbours in any way.

Many Japanese brides, some of them 'picture brides', came from Japan. They could not speak English and did not know Canadian customs, so Inouye and his followers organized a Japanese women's group. Mrs. Inouye taught the ladies to speak English, to cook in the Canadian way and also to learn Canadian table etiquette.

Around this time Mr. Yasutaro Yamaga, a man with leadership qualities, was assisting Mr. Inouye. Yasutaro Yamaga is perhaps one of the most well known among Japanese leaders — in the farming field, in adult education, in the co-operative union movement and in social work. They were both interested in Christianity and taught Sunday School at the Haney Corner Mission, which was inter-denominational and inter-racial in nature. In 1930, there were 160 Japanese and white Canadian children in attendance there. I introduced the Yamaga family to Rev. Yutaka Ogura of the New Westminster United Church (then known as the Methodist Church), who baptized the members of the family at their home in Haney, B.C. I was also at this service and became a life long friend of the Yamagas.

Yasutaro Yamaga was born in Toyohama-mura, Toyota-gun, Hiroshima-ken, Japan in 1886 and came to Canada in 1907 from Seattle where he had arrived previously on the S. Aki-Maru. At first he worked for the C.P.R., where he had an accident and suffered a finger injury. He saw Jiro

Inouye's advertisement and articles about how profitable agricultural ventures in the Fraser Valley were, so he went to Haney in 1908 and lived there until 1942. He married, and he and his wife, Fumi, were blessed with three sons and two daughters. Unfortunately, the eldest son, Shinji, became ill when he was an infant and was disabled for life. Their second son, Asao, died in a swimming accident in the Fraser River while trying to save his friend from drowning and the third son sustained an injury in an accident when he was working at a sawmill in Mission City, B.C. The eldest daughter, a nurse, died suddenly of a heart attack in Calgary. Shinji and Kazuko (Mrs. Onishi) are the only surviving children.

Yasutaro Yamaga was one of the rare older Japanese Canadians, who was able to speak English well and to understand the Canadian way of life. He shared Jiro Inouye's belief that in order to be accepted as a Canadian it was necessary to integrate. He worked diligently for this ideal to the end of his life.

The contributions Yamaga made to both Japanese and occidental Canadians alike are praiseworthy. He acted to clarify misunderstandings due to an inadequate understanding of English and to interpret for both the Japanese and the occidental people. For example, there was a "Sabbath Day" or "Lord's Day" Act which prohibited manual work on Sundays. The Japanese Canadian farmers in the Fraser Valley did not know about this law and would clear land with dynamite on Sundays. Of course deafening noises which followed annoyed the earnest church-going occidentals and they complained to Yamaga who had to tell the Japanese of the existing laws.

In order to help the Japanese people in Haney, the Haney Japanese Club, the Haney Japanese Women's Club, and the Haney Japanese Young People's Club were organized. Mr. Yamaga and his associates gave talks to the club members to promote better understanding of the Canadian way of life. The Japanese in Canada in those days lived just as they did in Japan — eating Japanese food such as tsukemono (pickled radish), miso-shiru (soybean soup), etc.; using Japanese dishes and eating with chopsticks. They did not use spoons, forks, knives, and they did not know about Canadian table manners because they lived a life isolated from the other Canadians. In Haney, the Japanese Women's Club started classes in cooking, sewing, knitting and English table manners, and English language lessons. However, the English-language course did not progress too well.

In the public schools, Japanese children could not speak much English and because of the cultural differences it was difficult for the Japanese children to understand the teachers and classmates. As the numbers of Japanese Canadian children in the public school increased they began to speak Japanese with each other and some of the white children learned to use very impolite Japanese words. When a Japanese person walked by, these children would shout, 'bakayaro!', which means 'you fool'. These children did not know the meaning of this word of abuse. Mr. Yamaga organized a Japanese P.T.A., and asked the parents to teach their children to stop this kind of bad language. He joined the public school P.T.A., and brought along some of the Japanese parents. And so in this way he was able to act as a bridge between the occidental and the Japanese Canadian communities.

With regard to the Japanese Language School in Haney, Jiro Inouye and Yasutaro Yamaga took special interest in the text books which were in use. In 1923, there were about thirty Japanese language schools in B.C. All these schools, excepting Haney's, were using the Japanese government text books. Many white Canadians believed that Japanese language schools were teaching Japanese nationalism which promoted militarism. In order to avoid any misunderstanding in their community, the Haney Japanese Language School used text books compiled by the Department of Education in the State of California, U.S.A. By countless other small but significant deeds Yamaga tried very hard to act as a bridge and peace maker.

As the number of strawberry growers increased, many

problems developed, such as overproduction, lack of markets, lack of price control for their produce, and above all the accelerating anti-Japanese sentiment. The occidental farmers, unable to compete with the Japanese, were blaming the Japanese for the low price of berries. In order to solve the many problems, Yamaga realized the importance of a united farmers' co-operative, and through his leadership the Maple Ridge Co-operative Produce Exchange was organized in 1926. Yasutaro Yamaga put all of his energy and knowledge into this co-operative which carried on successfully until the Second World War. The Co-op had a plant to receive and sell berries and other farm produce, a jam factory as well as a berry preserving plant. Barrelled berries were even sent to England.

Jiro Inouye passed away on October 6, 1931 at age 61 and two years later his wife went back to Japan with her adopted 12-year-old daughter. Yasutaro Yamaga carried on in the footsteps of Jiro Inouye and worked diligently for the welfare of Japanese Canadians.

With the start of the Pacific War, all Japanese organizations were ordered to stop operating and later properties, homes, automobiles, boats, etc., were confiscated and sold. Many farmers were sent by the Canadian government to Manitoba, and Southern Alberta, to work in the sugar beet industries, while others were relocated to the ghost towns in the interior of B.C. The Yamaga family was placed in Tashme, a newly created relocation camp near Hope, B.C. Yasutaro could not remain idle in this camp so he started a small sawmill, 14 miles from Tashme. When the war ended, he and his friend Chiaki Katsuno moved to the Cariboo district of B.C., and started a sawmill at 70 Mile House. Yamaga worked hard at this mill until he reached his 70th birthday.

I visited the camp one day and after an evangelistic meeting Mr. Yamaga said, "I will retire when I reach my 70th birthday, and I am planning to do something which will help some old and lonely Isseis." He did not mention what his plan was then. But as he foretold, he bought an orchard near the town of Beamsville, Ontario and there established a

Senior Citizen's Home for the elderly Japanese called Nipponia Home. It was not an easy task to make his vision of social service a reality as the majority of Japanese Canadians were still young and they could not see the need for a senior citizen's home. He gave practically all he had to build the home and also got some financial help from his wealthy relatives in Edmonton, Alberta, as well as the Ontario government. Finally, a lovely home for the Issei was built and in 1958 the first people moved in.

Mr. and Mrs. Yamaga and their eldest son, Shinji lived in Nipponia Home and shared with the 40 or so inhabitants their joys and sorrows. Unfortunately, Mr. and Mrs. Yamaga were involved in a motor vehicle accident in 1971 and as a result of this, their health weakened. Mr. Yamaga died on August 24, 1971 followed by Mrs. Yamaga in the same year.

We Japanese Canadians will always honour the Yamagas with a thankful heart.

Kozo Shimotakahara
First Japanese Canadian Physician

The following is the story of Dr. Shimotakahara, written by his daughter-in-law, Ruth, wife of the late Vernon Shimotakahara. She is now Mrs. Frank Penfold.

Kozo Shimotakahara was born Dec. 27, 1885 in Ibusuki-mura, Kagoshima-ken, Japan. Kagoshima-ken has a strange dialect of its own and is well known for its colorful and flamboyant personalities. His family was humble but an honourable one. His desire to emigrate to the west arose because his elder brother had gone to the U.S. to study medicine. His brother died, however of tuberculosis. Kozo resolved to fulfill his brother's dream and left Japan at the tender age of fourteen. His mother gave him her life savings, a mere 5 yen which she had saved from selling eggs, and she admonished him not to spend it except when he was in dire

55

Kozo Shimotakahara, 1930

need. He remembered the depths of his mother's love throughout his life. The family were devout Buddhists, and from them he had learned the value of regular worship. She advised him to go to church, even a Christian one, for by so doing he would be less vulnerable to evil influences. The miokuri or farewell scene was one he remembered all his life. All his friends, neighbours and relatives came to wish him well, and built bonfires on the shore. From the boat he saw the Kagoshima shoreline bright with fires and smoke trailing a farewell into the skies.

In 1900 a Japanese Methodist Church with Rev. G. Kaburagi as its minister, was in Vancouver. There was also a dormitory for those without families and homes, and consequently Kozo lived at that dormitory. Incidentally, he was its youngest occupant.

To realize his ambition to become a doctor, he had to learn the English language. He enrolled at Strathcona School to learn his A B C's. It must have been a comical sight to see a fourteen-year-old among the six-year-olds. However, his instructors were kind and encouraging. He studied by coal oil lamp and worked as a school boy domestic to support himself. His employers were often elderly people and though they were kind, he never had enough to eat. (Later in life, he commented that he believed that insufficient nourishment had robbed him of his full growth.) With special coaching, he completed grade school in four years.

His high school years were spent at Britannia High. Again he supported himself by working as a school boy for another elderly couple. They were kind to him, but could not provide a separate room for him, and he was forced by circumstances to sleep in the wood shed. How remarkable that he, too, did not become ill like his elder brother.

During the summer he worked in Steveston, as a fisherman's assistant. These fishermen were extremely wild and carefree. They drank copiously and gambled recklessly, for they had no purpose in life. It happened that the fisherman for whom he worked was very short-tempered, and no one wanted to work with him. But Kozo handled him wisely, and cooked delicious Japanese meals for him, such as tempura and chiri. He took care not to antagonize him and worked hard to please him. Kozo studied every spare moment he had, even on the fishing boats, and the fishermen were impressed with his diligence. In spite of the debauchery about him, Kozo did not succumb to these temptations. At the end of the summer, his partner was so pleased with Kozo that he gave him a full 50 percent of his profits. This was extremely generous, for Kozo had brought no investments with him, only his amiability and eagerness to work.

Immigration of the Japanese came in two distinct stages. The first was during the period 1885-1910. It was composed predominantly of adult males who were mostly farmers, fishermen and labourers. They were attracted to British Columbia because of its proximity to Japan and similarity to their native land. Its natural beauties — majestic mountains, verdant forests, rugged shoreline and rushing rivers appealed to them. Many of the fish caught in these waters were similar to those caught in Japan. It was natural that many of them turned to fishing for their livelihood. Being bachelors their lives were very carefree and mobile.

The contacts of these Japanese immigrants with the Caucasian population was mostly in economic competition. The fact that the Japanese were willing, as well as forced, to work for lower wages and longer working hours, threatened to undermine the standard of living of the white or Caucasian population. This was a major factor in creating the beginning of racial prejudice against the Japanese.

In the fall, he continued his high school studies and his housework. During the last year of his high school, he worked for Mr. and Mrs. J. Malkin of Shaughnessy Heights, Vancouver, B.C. Mr. Malkin was an eminent Vancouver businessman, and his was a devout Christian home. They were extremely kind to Kozo and called him John. Through witnessing their daily lives he learned to appreciate the true meaning of Christianity. He worked for them until his graduation in June 1908.

He enrolled at Columbian College, a Christian college in New Westminster. Being bilingual, he was able to secure full time work using his language skills. It was at New Westminster that he met Rev. Y. Akagawa, who was to become his life long friend. Through the influence of the college, he was moved to apply to become a medical missionary, but for some unknown reason was turned down.

In summer, he continued to work with the fishermen to earn money for his living expenses and tuition. He graduated in June 1911.

He then attended the University of Chicago Medical School where he experienced further hardships. He worked at various jobs, as a waiter at a Chinese restaurant, as a cook and baker to a wealthy family, and as a houseboy to a wealthy bachelor. At times he could not keep awake in class, and as a result one of his professors made him sit in the very front row. He even worked as a red-cap porter on a train during the summer. Again many examples of Christian thoughtfulness on the part of his employers were shown to him. Sometimes the employer would inform his guests that his houseboy was working his way through school, and they would kindly slip him some money. At another time, his bachelor employer closed his window during a violent rain storm because Kozo had fallen asleep.

Finally after four arduous years, he graduated from medical school in June 1915. In later years Kozo remarked that he didn't know how he did it.

Even then, his problems were not over. He did not have the funds to buy a graduation gown, and so his employer kindly bought one for him.

His graduation was a happy but lonely one, for he did not have a family and well-wishers as other graduates. When he returned to his room, he turned to the East-symbolically Japan, and reported to his parents his successful graduation. Both his parents had died a few years before. His mother appeared to him in a white kimono, in a dream; the white kimino signified funeral attire. He worked again to earn funds for his train fare to the west coast.

He went to a hotel in Seattle, Washington, whose proprietor was Mr. Higo, to prepare for his exams to obtain medical licenses to practice in the United States, the State of Washington, Japan, and British Columbia. While there, he visited Dr. M. Obayashi, to pay his respects, and there he met Obayashi's sister-in-law, Miss Shin Kusama, who later became Kozo's wife. Dr. Obayashi was minister at the Seattle Japanese Church. Rev. Y. Akagawa urged Kozo to marry Shin, and arranged that they should see more of each other by inviting Shin to stay at the Akagawa home. They became engaged.

Miss Kusama returned to Seattle and worked for a Japanese doctor so that she could learn the ins and outs of a doctor's office. They were engaged for six months during which time they corresponded in English. Most Issei do not have sufficient command of the English language to correspond in that tongue. Thus their courtship was unusual because of this fact.

Kozo passed his State of Washington exam with first class honors. In fact he passed all his exams successfully. He could have practiced anywhere in the United States, but he had been persuaded to practice in Vancouver, B.C. for there was no licenced Japanese doctor at that time.

They were married June 5, 1916, and honeymooned by boat to Victoria. They were unable to travel further because of lack of funds, and returned with just two dollars remaining.

He started his practice in a small room of the Japanese Church and Kozo and Shin boarded at the dormitory. After awhile his increasing practice necessitated moving to larger quarters. For this he rented an entire building at Powell and Main streets for just $30 a month. How low the rents were in those days! Later he bought this building. To cut down on expenses they made their living quarters this building too. Convalescing patients who had no other place to go, also stayed and were nursed by Shin. The facilities were very inadequate and made for much extra work. Those were the conditions under which Dr. K. Shimotakahara started his practice.

Because Japan was an ally during World War I and had risen in prestige among the world powers as a result of its victory over the Russians, the Canadian government was not as severe in restricting the immigration of Japanese as they were the Chinese. The government negotiated a Gentleman's Agreement with Japan whereby only 350 of the laboring class would be admitted. Unlike the Chinese, the Japanese were permitted to bring or send for Japanese women from Japan to become their wives. During the period 1907 to 1920 there were more adult Japanese women immigrants than Japanese males.

Consequently, the whole pattern of their settlement became different. The Japanese couples raised families and became a part of their community. The Chinese men in contrast, were forced to lead bachelors' existences and many wandered about from place to place. Others being family men sent money to their families and relatives in China and thus further reduced their standard of living. This basic difference has accounted for some of the dissimilar manners in which the two Oriental groups became settled in Canada.

Thus at the time when Kozo started his practice, there was already a sizeable Japanese community. It is regrettable that they did not disperse to wider areas but settled close to Vancouver. In 1921 there was one Oriental to every thirteen Caucasians, and at that time the people in B.C. were fearing that it was becoming a problem of which race would predominate in British Columbia.

Shortly after he had started his practice, the First World War began. Kozo aspired to become an army doctor, and Shin gave him her blessing. However, for some reason he was rejected.

His rejection was fortunate for the Japanese community because he was to render them his first great service soon after. The terrible flu epidemic of 1918 came to B.C. The Vancouver General Hospital was full to capacity, and it was difficult to find a place that would take patients with flu. Because of their language inadequacy, it was kinder and necessary to place Japanese patients among people who could communicate with them. Through the efforts of Rev. Y. Akagawa and Consul K. Ukita, it was arranged that Strathcona School would be borrowed from the authorities for three weeks, and made into a temporary hospital. This was October 1918 and continued until November. All schools were closed because of the flu epidemic. As a result of the fear of the disease it was extremely difficult to get volunteers to nurse the patients. Mrs. Akagawa, wife of the minister, a former nurse, was placed in charge, and trained the volunteers who were Mrs. Higashi, wife of Rev. Higashi, Mrs. Nakano, a former Red Cross nurse in Japan, Mrs. G. Yatabe and Mrs. Ishii, housewives and young mothers. They worked a staggering twelve hours, from seven a.m. to seven p.m. It was exhausting work, especially for those who had never done nursing before, and also frightening and heart breaking, for some of the patients were so seriously ill that they died. These were the days before antibiotic medicines. Dr. Shimotakahara, Dr. Sato, Dr. Ishiwara, and Dr. Kinoshita volunteered their services. As before Dr. Shimotakahara was the only licensed Japanese doctor who could legally prescribe the necessary medicines. He was greatly praised for his tireless efforts in caring for the flu patients. By setting up such a temporary isolation hospital, many patients were assured recovery and others were spared contagion.

It is interesting to note that the bulk of the volunteer work at this temporary hospital was done by Japanese Christians. Some had been newly converted to Christianity, and had been inspired to show it tangibly by aiding their fellow man.

Because so many of the Japanese Issei as well as their children attended or had attended Strathcona School, it was decided that it would be an excellent thing for its principal, Mr. Elmer Brown, to see first hand the country from which these people originally came. Having visited their native land, he would be more informed and sympathetic to them, and could help to promote better understanding between the Japanese people and the British Columbia public. Dr. K.

Shimotakahara was active also in helping to raise the necessary funds.

His practice grew and prospered. Several deserving Japanese Canadian students were given moral support and lent money by him, for he remembered his own early hardships.

He became a respected and influential leader in the Japanese Methodist Church, and was generous financially in supporting it. Ministers such as Rev. Y. Akagawa, Rev. Y. Yoshioka, and Rev. Y. Ogura always knew that they could count on him for entertainment and a delicious meal whenever they were in town. When he couldn't be present, he sent his nephew, Tetsuo to be host to them.

He was especially interested in guiding young people to church; he felt that foundations for a good life are laid when young. He often treated the young people to Chinese dinners after church, and some attended only because they liked a good Chinese meal. However, many of these same people today, admit to his wisdom for they say that his early influence has helped to guide them into becoming responsible human beings.

The idea of forming a Japanese clinic was initiated by the Japanese United Church under the leadership of Rev. K. Shimizu in May 1932. The clinic was located on Pender East and was operated once a week for those patients who could not afford the services of a private physician. It was supported entirely by donations of money, medicine and time. World War II brought an end to its services. Again Dr. K. Shimotakahara was one of the guiding influences behind the project. Dr. M. Uchida, Dr. Shimokura, and Dr. H. Kamitakahara gave their services voluntarily also. Many women from the Japanese Church and others from Japanese Women's organizations volunteered their time. Mrs. T. Hyodo was elected President of the Auxiliary. These ladies helped with the paper work and aided in obtaining necessary supplies such as linen. They also made arrangements to show films explaining the cause and cure of tuberculosis. Two nurses who were most generous with their time were Miss

Ruth Akagawa and Miss Louise Tsuchiya. Mr. E. Kagetsu donated a much needed portable x-ray.

There was also an oriental hospital on Powell Street under the auspices of the Catholic Church. Its primary purpose was to detect and treat t.b. among the Japanese and Chinese patients. Dr. K. Shimotakahara was often called to help in consultation. Largely through his efforts, the hospital was presented with an x-ray machine valued at $3,500. A Mr. Inamoto, a prominent industrialist from Japan, was greatly impressed with Dr. Shimotakahara's contribution to the oriental community and had agreed to send the x-ray machine to Vancouver from Japan.

Kozo was greatly concerned with the rising rate of tuberculosis among the Japanese, and especially among the farming folk. He attributed its increase to the Depression. Thus through arrangements with the Welfare Dept. of Vancouver, he took films on tuberculosis and venereal disease to the outlying districts of new Westminster, Port Haney, Mission City, Hammond and Strawberry Hill, all of which were farming communities. He showed these films at the Japanese Language School in Vancouver, the Japanese School at Fairview, at Fanny Bay where the Kagetsu logging camp was located and at Woodfibre, a paper and pulp mill town. Distant places had to be reached by boat and train, the expense of which he paid himself. Miss Ruth Akagawa, a nurse, often accompanied him as did his nephew Tetsuo Kamitakahara who ran the projector. It must be remembered that many of the Issei did not have a command of the English language, and it was only through his commentaries in Japanese that information could be disseminated. Often these sessions did not end until midnight, and thus these excursions took two days. He held clinics on Sunday after church at these centers once a month.

Gradually during the twenties there was a shift in the kind of occupations of the Japanese. They moved into farming and occupations of a commercial and service nature because fishing, lumbering, mining and railroading jobs became scarce, and because there was discrimination against them in these industries. They became clerks, proprietors of stores, restaurants, rooming houses, or went into businesses and professions.

Dr. I. Niitobe attended the Pacific Conference at Banff, Alberta in 1933. On his return to Japan in October of that year, he passed through Vancouver, and was stricken with leukemia at Victoria, B.C. The Japanese consulate issued urgent calls for blood and asked Dr. Shimotakahara to supervise the testing. About one hundred people volunteered to give their blood, and consequently he closed his office to his regular practice for two days to test blood types. Only about three of the necessary type "B" was found. Blood type "A" is most frequently found among the Japanese. Arrangements and fares for the donors to go to Victoria were paid by the Consulate, but it was too late. Dr. Niitobe died that same day on Oct. 12, 1933.

In 1940, the celebration of the year 2600 in Japan, Kozo was presented with a lacquered sakazuki (a sake cup) with the Imperial Crest, as recognition of his outstanding service to the Japanese people.

Then came World War II and Pearl Harbor. The Japanese were informed that they would be evacuated en masse from the coast. The Custodian notified Kozo that the office would collect any fees owed him. However, he felt it would be heartless to demand his fees through this office. He could have made himself richer by $15,000 by collecting from his patients who could pay. But, after Pearl Harbor, because of his compassion for his fellow Japanese, he again sacrificed personal gain and cancelled medical debts owed him by the Japanese.

After Pearl Harbor, the Japanese were interned in Hastings Park, Vancouver, B.C. That was a most difficult time for all Japanese for they were filled with fears of the future. There were illnesses resulting from tensions and apprehensions and from the crowded manner in which they were forced to live. For that reason it was an especially difficult time for doctors. All the Japanese doctors worked tirelessly and gratuitously. Dr. Shimotakahara, being most well-known, was called the most frequently. He attended his people daily and late into the night.

Like the other Japanese doctors, he was moved inland. Because of his seniority, he was appointed to Kaslo as this center had the least number of Japanese evacuees — that is 2,000 Japanese. Like the other Japanese doctors he received a salary of a mere $100 a month. The B.C. Security Commission however, did provide a house which they maintained by supplying fuel, fire wood and electricity.

Once a month he visited Lemon Creek and the Slocan projects to assist Dr. Hiroshi Kamitakara. Dr. H. Kuwabara was the physician at Sandon, and Dr. M. Uchida at New Denver.

It was not easy to administer to the folk at these projects for they were living under most trying conditions. But his kindness and good humor often helped his patients more than any medication he could prescribe for them.

The Doukhobors and other Caucasians living in the environs began to come too, for they had heard of the effectiveness of his treatments. His specialty was the treatment of arthritis. Patients came to him from as far away as Alberta.

In 1946 he went east to Montreal with the intention of studying pathology. It was unfortunate that so many years ago when he was preparing for the other examinations, he had not taken an exam which would have enabled him to practice in all Canada. He studied conscientiously in an old overstuffed chair in a basement in Verdun, Montreal, but pathology was quite different in 1946. Kozo was 61 years of age. However, his example inspired an Issei friend to study bookkeeping, and this friend was successful in finding employment as a bookkeeper. That an Issei was able to hold such a position was a remarkable feat.

Thus it was that Kozo returned to Kaslo, B.C. with the intention of making his permanent residence there. He had a house built. It was fortunate, indeed, for an interior town to have the services of such a doctor. Though in later years most of the Japanese had relocated elsewhere, he had once again built up a thriving practice among Caucasians.

In the course of his practice he met a boy, David Dryden who came to him as a patient. David was much puzzled about his future for he was dissatisfied with the odd jobs he had held. He decided to become a minister, and in his testimonial as to why he had chosen that career, he explained that Dr. Shimotakahara had always encouraged him, and had urged him to complete his Junior and Senior matriculation. It was through his influence that he had been led to study for the ministry.

Even in his sixties, Kozo went boldly on making plans for the future. One of his cherished hopes was another Japanese clinic in the east which would be served by all the Japanese doctors.

Because of the prejudice encountered by the Issei, they reasoned that the best way to buck discrimination was through education of their children. Thus a very high percentage of the Nisei were enrolled in correspondence courses, vocationl schools, colleges and universities and graduated from them. Consequently many of them were well equipped when they relocated to Eastern Canada to fill well paid, responsible and satisfying positions. At this stage of the history of the Japanese in Canada, there were now the Sansei (third) and even the Yonsei (fourth) generation. As an immigrant group, they have generally attained a high standard of living.

The year 1951 was a very eventful one for Kozo and his wife. In January of that year, just when the road conditions were at their worst, he received an urgent early morning telephone call from near Mirror Lake, B.C. In going to see his patient, Kozo's car skidded and fell sixty feet, almost into the lake. He was discovered wandering in shock, by a Greyhound bus driver, and taken home in a taxi by a friend and patient. His injuries were discovered to be a broken collar bone and the loss of a few teeth. It was a miracle that he was not hurt more severely or that he had not been killed. Under doctor's orders he was warned to rest completely for two weeks. But Kozo could not remain quiet, and he was discovered by his doctor going to see patients. Finally, Shin had

67

to accept his inability to remain home, and carrying his black bag for him, she accompanied him on his house calls.

Then on April 1, 1951, they received another early morning telephone call informing him that his newphew Dr. Hiroshi Kamitakahara had died suddenly. His death came as a great shock for Kozo for he had loved him as a son, and had sent him through medical school. He had hoped that Hiroshi would take over his practice someday upon his retirement. After the funeral at Greenwood, B.C., Kozo became despondent and returned to Kaslo in a dazed condition. He could not write. The doctor diagnosed his condition as that of an extreme nervous breakdown. He was hospitalized at the Kaslo Victoria Hospital for about a month. Having been advised to have a complete change of scenery, Kozo decided to visit his sons and their families in Montreal. His friends in the east gave him a thirty-fifth wedding anniversary party. They urged him to see the wonders of New York City, and he had a happy and carefree time there with his son, Vernon. After a complete physical check-up, he was declared in excellent shape for a man of his years. He motored back across the country and saw the wonderful scenery of the United States and Canada.

Thus he was in the best of spirits when he again resumed his practice in Kaslo. However, in mid-November while attending a patient who had suffered a heart attack, he himself had a fainting spell. Later it was diagnosed as his first heart attack. After that he often complained of being fatigued, but he insisted on making house calls, seeing his patients at the hospital as well as at the clinic. On Nov. 30, his last day on earth, he performed two tonsillectomies in the morning and put in a very long day at the clinic until seven p.m. He returned home too tired to eat, and soon after had another and fatal heart attack. Thus expired this brave and tender man on November 30, 1951.

He was survived by his wife and two sons, Vernon and George, an ear, nose and throat specialist, and his daughter Sachi-Jean.

Kaslo was shocked to hear of his passing for he had

been such a well-known and beloved citizen of that town. On the appointed day all stores in Kaslo closed that all might attend his funeral. In a eulogy from the *Kootenian* paper, come the words of E. J. Leveque, "Were all to whom he performed a special service to bring a blossom to his grave, he would sleep tonight under an avalanche of flowers".

The townspeople in seeking a fitting memorial to him, decided to create a Dr. K. Shimotakahara Children's Ward at the Victoria Hospital. It was realized entirely through voluntary contributions.

His life is truly a Horatio Alger story. It is reassuring to learn that in Canada a person however humble his origin, can attain his dream if he really wants to succeed and is willing to make the necessary sacrifices to attain his goal.

Dr. Kozo Shimotakahara was a wise counselor and generous leader of his people. On the other hand, he possessed the normal interests of other men. He was an ardent fisherman, and with his friends and relatives frequently arose at early dawn to pursue this sport. He also had an aviary and enjoyed feeding and admiring his birds before going to the office. He was a born comic and was often the "life of a party". He possessed elements of greatness but also had human weaknesses and faults.

But his many services and kindnesses to his patients attest to his conscientiousness and integrity of character. Always he did his very best for them. His life will serve as an inspiration to others for he emanated his Christian belief in his daily living.

He experienced life in its fullest — heady success as well as bitter defeat. He saw human beings at their finest and when they were most contemptible, but through it all he remained a noble soul who loved his fellow man.

Denbei Kobayashi with his
chrysanthemums, Oct 1945

Denbei Kobayashi
Poet and Farmer

There are many beautiful lakes in Canada, especially in British Columbia, and Okanagan Lake is one of them. It extends from Penticton to Vernon for about ninety miles. I spent several summers from the early 1920's at Mr. Takataro Tada's farm in Summerland, B.C., and through him I was introduced to Mr. Denbei Kobayashi, a gentleman, poet, teacher and farmer.

Denbei Kobayashi and his wife, Hiro, were the much respected and loved leaders of a small group of Japanese orchard farmers. Their home was a haven of hospitality and was often used as a community meeting place. It was situated on a farm overlooking Okanagan Lake and had a lovely view.

Denbei Kobayashi was not only a leader of the Japanese community at Okanagan Centre but also of those who loved haiku (Japanese poems). He taught many to write haiku and through such cultural activities diverted them away from gambling which was rampant in the 1920's.

He was born in 1878, the second son of Tomezo and Kin Kobayashi, in Nishimura, Chisagata-gun, Nagano-ken, Japan. After graduating from the intermediate school of the village at age eleven, he helped to care for younger children. Later when he was old enough, he worked at a silk factory and travelled all over Japan selling silk-worm eggs. He also worked at a gold mine in Hokkaido and finally in 1906 set sail on a Canadian Pacific steamship for Canada and landed in Vancouver, B.C. He wanted to go to the United States of America but found that if he went fishing on the Skeena River he could make at least one thousand dollars in two months — so he went fishing. He worked very hard but his partner gambled and drank away both their shares so Mr. Kobayashi received nothing for his efforts. He went back to Vancouver with empty hands and as he could not live without money, joined the C.P.R. work gang. The leaders of the group were Koshiro Hamano and Yoshitsugu Ono. The work gang was sent to the C.P.R. Okanagan branch line. After

71

working at Enderby, they were moved to the mainline at Sicamous, where they were engaged in the dangerous and exhausting work of blasting rocks for the new railway. When winter arrived, they could not work, and lived in an entirely inadequate boxcar at Notch Hill Siding, suffering in the forty degrees below zero conditions. In the spring of 1907 the work gang moved back to the Okanagan branch line near Vernon after they finished blasting rocks.

One day they visited a big orchard at Cold Stream which employed a group of Japanese workers. The boss of this camp was Mr. Eijiro Koyama. Denbei Kobayashi and his friend Osuke Takizawa were hired by the Cold Stream Ranch and their wages were $1.40 a day for ten hours of work. They started to work on March 25, 1907 and Denbei's younger brother, Kizo, came to Canada as an immigrant in 1907 and joined them at Cold Stream after working for a time with the C.P.R work gang. The Cold Stream orchard employed more than forty Japanese and many were the people from his native prefecture of Nagano. Heiji Yamazaki, Takataro Tada, Sugitaro Sugiyama, Shimanosuke Kagegawa, Shumpei Totoki, Tenichi Komatsu, and others joined this group. Denbei Kobayashi learned how to care for young fruit trees, that is, grafting and pruning procedures, etc. As winter approached, there was no work for the men so most of the newcomers left the orchard, leaving the original few.

An accident occurred in July, 1907 that was remembered with amusement. The Honourable Chonosuke Yada, the Consul of Japan in Vancouver, came to visit the Japanese immigrants in the Okanagan area, but arrived at the Cold Stream Ranch earlier than expected. The people of the camp did not have enough time to prepare for a proper welcome. They asked the camp cook to make something special, and a sponge cake was baked in a great hurry. When the cake was brought in, they discovered many black spots in it. Mr. Kobayashi found that these were black ants which were in the flour. He apologized to the Japanese Consul, but the Consul smiled and said, "It's all right, this cake is delicious and I was told that if you eat ants you get strength."

KOBAYASHI

Denbei Kobayashi was naturalized as a Canadian citizen in April, 1908, and after two years in the Cold Stream orchard, he went to work in another orchard in the village called Oyama. This village was so named after a very famous Japanese, General Oyama, who was renowned as a great hero of the Sino-Japanese war. After working in Oyama, he moved to Okanagan Centre and made fences around the big Okanagan Valley Land Company orchard. A worker for this project could earn $2.50 per day while many were unemployed due to the depression. Even the ones who were lucky enough to have jobs were only being paid a dollar a day.

He was awarded the labor contract to plant 800 acres of fruit at Winfield by the Okanagan Valley Land Co. This project took three years, and some of the workers are still living in the Okanagan.

In 1913, Mr. Kobayashi went to Japan and was engaged to Hiro Yanagisawa. They were married on February 5, 1914, and the newly married couple left Japan on March 17, 1914. Tired after travelling by ship, train, boat and on foot, they finally came to Okanagan Centre. A reception party was held for them the following day by Mr. Fukumoto, the camp members from the Rainbow Ranch, and others. After the reception, Mrs. Kobayashi had to start work as the cook of the Okanagan Valley Land Company camp.

Interested in Japanese plants, Kobayashi brought early cherry blossom trees (higan sakura), Japanese peonies (botan), persimmons (kaki), bamboo, coltsfoot (fuki) and Japanese asparagus (udo) from Japan. Due to the severe winter conditions, all plants died except the sakura, fuki and udo. The early cherry blossom trees reproduced and he sent plants to many parts of Canada. Today, the blossoming cherry trees are enjoyed and admired by visitors to the many Canadian parks and boulevards in the spring.

The fruit trees which six Japanese workers planted under the supervision of Denbei Kobayashi on the eight hundred acre orchard of the Okanagan Valley Land Company at Okanagan Centre, grew and later bore beautiful fruit which is still being harvested for the benefit of all Canadians.

A few years after their marriage, the Kobayashis were blessed with a son and a daughter. They faced difficulty in raising their children in the crowded camp, so they bought a ten acre farm at Okanagan Centre and in the summer of 1914, they moved there. At the same time, the First World War started and his neighbour, a white man, enlisted so Denbei looked after his neighbour's twelve acre orchard for him. When the war ended, his neighbour returned and found the orchard in good order. Soon after, Mr. and Mrs. Kobayashi started working their farm at the Centre. By 1921, many Japanese moved into the area. In the same year, an association called 'Koyukai' (Friends and Fellowship Association) was formed. The first director and officers were Eijiro Koyama, president; Kakujiro Kaide, secretary; Denbei Kobayashi, chairman; and six others as directors. At the annual meeting in 1922, Denbei was elected president and held this office for thirteen years. While he was president, the organization published a monthly bulletin called *Taiko No Kishi (Shores of the Great Lake)* and during this time he and nine other haiku enthusiasts established another association called the Aoba Kai. In 1962, the Aoba Kai celebrated its fortieth anniversary by publishing a book of haiku.

In 1924, the Kobayashis bought their neighbour's seventeen acre orchard for $15,000 and settled down to bringing up their family in their new home. They now had three sons and four daughters and were doing very well with their business.

In 1958, the residents of Okanagan centre gave him the honour of planting the Centennial oak (blue spruce), an event which is marked for posterity with a bronze plaque.

Unfortunately, Mrs. Kobayashi had become ill with a stroke a few years earlier and was bedridden for six long years. She was cheerful in spite of her illness and her husband did his very best to care for her. She had a fatal stroke in May, 1960 and passed away peacefully on July 18, 1960. Mr. Kobayashi retired from farming in 1961, and transferred ten acres of his property to his son, Hiroshi, and twelve acres to Sakuji and Sachiyo Koyama, his son-in-law and daughter respectively. He visited Japan several times in the 1960's. He published his autobiography and a collection of his haiku in 1963. In 1966 he was honoured with a silver medal and a citation for his contribution to the development of agriculture by Prince Takamatsu of Japan. His contribution as a leader of his community and teacher of haiku will not be forgotten by his many friends.

Denbei Kobayashi peacefully passed away on January 4, 1968 at the age of eighty-nine.

Kichinozo Imayoshi
Fruit Grower

Mr. Jack Kichinozo Imayoshi, who lives in Summerland, B.C., told me his story as a pioneer fruit grower in Okanagan, B.C. The following is in his words.

I have no written record of my life in Canada, but I will tell you some of the happenings as I remember them. This year (1982), I will be ninety-two years old. My son, Isamu and I are fruit farmers and I still work in the orchard. We have thirty acres of mixed fruit orchard such as peaches, apricots, cherries, plums and pears. We have early, middle and later crops, beginning with cherries followed by apricots, peaches, plums, pears and ending with apples.

In 1948, I became a naturalized Canadian citizen and my wife was naturalized in 1952. We vote proudly at each election now, but back in 1907 when I first arrived, things were not as they are today. The sudden arrival of Japanese immigrants must have helped foment the anti-Japanese mob that attacked the Japanese community around Powell Street in Vancouver in 1907. I did not encounter this mob, as I was already working for Kinji Ohama's C.P.R. gang in Medicine Hat, Alberta, making fifteen cents per hour. When winter arrived that year there was no further work so we returned to

Vancouver. We looked for employment but could not find any so we spent our time in a Japanese hotel.

In the spring of 1908, Mr. Matsumoto, the proprietor of the hotel, had a brush clearing job in Prince Rupert which he had contracted from the Grand Trunk Railway. I went to Prince Rupert with a friend to look for work but was unsuccessful so we again returned to Vancouver. Fortunately, we were able to find a land clearing job in North Vancouver and for a short time we worked there. When we were finished with our work here I found a job through a Japanese agent in Vancouver and went to work for an irrigation ditch building camp in Vernon, B.C. I went to Vernon in July or August and worked there until the spring of 1909. After that I again worked on a C.P.R. gang — Mr. Shintani's. We received twenty cents per hour wages. There were some gamblers in this group and I foolishly joined them and lost money. I realized the danger of continuing to be with these people, and sought other employment. A friend, Mr. Y. Ageno, told me of a ditch digging job in Summerland, so I went there in April. I worked in both Summerland and Kelowna until 1916 — working in the orchard during summer and cutting fuel wood during winter. The wages were twenty cents per hour. My living quarters were either a tent or a shack and I had to cook my meals as well. Some of the time I worked at a sawmill, cutting logs for fifty cents an hour which was the highest wage in those days.

In 1917, with two other Japanese friends we farmed on a shared basis — dividing our profits and expenses equally. We planted tomatoes, and onions, but because of a poor crop we only made $350 — one ton of tomatoes for a cannery was $13 and one hundred pounds of onion was only $2.

In 1918, I began growing fruit and vegetables with another friend in Summerland, renting a field from a white Canadian neighbour. On May 24, 1918, a heavy frost hit most crops in the area but fortunately, our farm escaped severe damages, and we survived harvesting a good crop that year. At the end of the year my friend and I bought ten acres of land for $5,000. We paid $2,000 cash and the remaining

$3,000 was to be paid as soon as we were able to at an interest rate of eight per cent annually. However, we found this land was unsuitable for fruit growing so we rented more land and grew vegetables. We took ten years, using profits from the vegetables crops in our rented farm, to pay for our ten acres.

I went to Japan at the end of 1919 to get married, and came back to Summerland in February, 1920. Our eldest son was born on December 27, 1920. We are blessed with five children born between 1920 and 1930.

After we paid for our property in full in 1929, a white Canadian farmer wanted to exchange his property for ours so I gave him $2,000 and our property and we got his which our family now owns. We became self supporting farmers around 1930. I found that the fruit in our new property was not good enough for market, so decided that we needed another farm. In 1934, a land next to ours was put up for sale by the village. I asked for the land but the village refused to sell it to me because I was Japanese. I asked my Canadian friend to buy the land in his name and then bought it from him. The price of that land was $300. We cleared the land and planted apples and soft fruit, and grew vegetables in between the rows. We had good crops but because of the depression we were unable to sell the produce. After the depression we harvested good crops but in 1959 a heavy frost damaged the cherries and peaches. Cold spells came again in 1961 and 1965 and all the fruit trees were killed, so we had to pull out all the trees. The Canadian government helped all of us Okanagan orchard owners financially so I am grateful.

In the early days there were no organized shippers in the Okanagan area. Independent shippers gathered the fruit from growers and shipped them to the prairie markets by consignment. The wholesalers in the prairies sometimes sold the fruit at very low prices causing the growers to suffer. The apples shipped in 1919 brought almost no return to the growers.

In 1920, the B.C. Fruit Growers' Association was formed and an expert on co-op management was hired. A great movement got under way to unify the growers in the

Okanagan Valley. This was the beginning of the co-op in this area. However, there were independent shippers who did not join the B.C. Fruit Growers' Association and who gathered fruit from the farmers and sold them on consignment basis as before so there was confusion on the market.

During the years 1934 and 1935 the Co-op bought the packing houses of independent dealers, and sold the fruit through one organization, the B.C. Fruit Growers' Association, so that the market became more stable. We had previously sent our fruit by railway to the prairie market, but truck transportation was much easier and simpler. The trucks came directly to the farms and carried the fruit directly to the prairie wholesalers. The independent dealers hindered the unifying of market prices.

I feel that fruit growers in the Okanagan Valley need to study how to sell their produce as well as how to grow their crops more efficiently. The government has now established a crop insurance plan which means that growers will be assured of funds in case of crop failures due to adverse weather conditions. Since 1975, the crop insurance plan has covered losses when market prices do not cover the cost production. Therefore, our occupation is a more stable one.

I was born the eldest son of a poor farmer at Kagoshima, Japan in 1890, having six brothers. When I became eighteen, I decided to come to North America. My motive was to gain money and to help my family. In addition, as I did not desire life in the army, I avoided conscription by coming to Canada. In April 1907, I landed in Hawaii. I really wanted to come to the mainland of the United States of America but the American government prohibited Japanese immigrants from entering. I believe this was an attempt to deal with the anti-Japanese sentiment, particularly regarding Japanese children in public schools. As I wished to come to the North American mainland I came to Vancouver by ship with other Japanese.

Although my plan was to earn some money and return to Japan, I have now lived in Canada for seventy-five years and have been a fruit grower for over sixty years. Summerland is my second native place — my real home.

All our children are well and living here — contributing to Canadian society through their chosen occupations. We love Canada, a land rich in natural resources, and a country which cares for the poor and the weak. We thank God for this peaceful Canada.

One of the Imayoshi children, Kutch, became a Baptist minister. He has added some words to his father's story.

Like many of the Japanese who came to Canada in the early 1900's, my father was a very industrious worker. This was absolutely necessary just to survive. Hard work was inbred in us very early in our lives: I can clearly remember working like a slave cutting down huge pine trees, hauling out tons of rocks and stones to clear the land in order to plant fruit trees; and picking hundreds of boxes of tomatoes, cantaloups, eggplants, peaches, pears, cherries and apples from early morning to late at night.

My father's many years of sacrificial labour has resulted in some modest accomplishments; thirty acres of orchard and a comfortable home, free of debt; five children, all grown, who can thank him for his example of thrift, hard work, and dedication to the task — an example which has enabled his children to receive an appropriate education and good guidance.

While this story is about my father, nevertheless our mother, who also is living and well, played a large role both on the farm and in the upbringing of the children.

Another factor which influenced my father's life was his involvement in the local Japanese United Church congregation. Although the congregation has remained quite small in numbers, it has had a good influence upon the Japanese community and my father continues to take an active part in the church.

In 1982, at ninety-two years of age, he considers himself fortunate to enjoy relatively good health and he is happy that he is still able to spend his days working in the orchard, driving the tractor. Without that interest, his life would be indeed very empty.

Kumagai Family

Mrs. Misa Kumagai, James Akira,
Makio, Mr. Zenjuro Kumagai, Paul Sakae

Kumagai Family

The following story sent by Dr. Paul Kumagai of New Westminster is included here as his tribute to his family and friends but particularly to his mother.

On December 5, 1873 my dad, Zenjuro Kumagai, was born in the small town of Ishinomori, Miyagi-ken, Japan. He was purported to be a direct descendant of the fiftieth emperor of Japan, Kammutenno (737-806 A.D.). His more recent ancestor was Sodenoyama, the grand sumo wrestling champion of the Shogun era.

At a young age he was sent to a private school in the same village but his stepfather took him out after two years and made him work at a factory.

At twenty-one he married Miss Komatsu, the eldest daughter of a noble family in a neighbouring village.

There was a family feud in connection with the successor to the estate; Dad was very upset and left home to come to Canada in 1897. His ambition was to work hard and become a successful businessman. He was humble, calm and patient but not aggressive enough to get ahead in a competitive world. He could neither read, write nor speak English. Fortunately his English neighbours helped him to improve his English.

In 1903, Dad became a Canadian by naturalization so he could own a boat and fish on the Fraser River. Fishing was good in those days and he was able to catch a boatload in four or five hours.

From spring to fall he spent most of his time fishing and in winter he worked at a local lumber mill in Fraser Mills which was on the banks of the Fraser River.

When Mother came to Canada in 1904, Dad purchased a few acres of land across the road from the Vancouver Country and Golf course. Dad was a good-natured fellow with a big heart and often helped the recently-arrived immigrants from Japan. At times there were twenty or thirty people staying at our place. The immigrants helped by making a good-sized fruit and vegetable garden. They also built recreational facilities such as a gym for wrestling, judo, kendo and weight lifting, enabling everyone to take part in sports, especially in the winter months. Activities also included reading books, magazines and newspapers and playing cards and checker games.

My older brother Makio was born in 1905 and I was born in 1907. There were no other children in the neighbourhood and so our playmates were small black baby bears which came to look for food every day, and three big dogs. It was great fun.

Mother became ill with rheumatism and arthritis which doctors diagnosed as fatal. Subsequently, Dad sold everything and we all went back to Japan. Dad took many interesting articles from Canada such as a hammock, lanterns to use at night, especially in stormy weather, and a small pistol for protection. He bought musical and singing clocks in Tokyo. All these articles were novel in Dad's home town.

Father operated a big farm in the town of Ishinomori. As well, he made noodles on a commercial basis. His ambition was too great as he lacked experience and organizational skills and eventually went bankrupt.

Miraculously Mother began to improve and so Dad decided to return to Canada and re-establish himself by working hard. Between fishing and lumbering he saved enough money to call us back to Canada. When we arrived in New Westminster, there was a strong anti-Japanese movement here because many Japanese immigrants did not behave well. They spent their time gambling, drinking, fighting, and there were even gun battles.

While in Japan we had to go to school. I was very lucky for I enjoyed everything about school, the teachers and the subjects. In 1921 I was chosen as one of the four most outstanding students in all Japan and received a special certificate of proficiency. Dad had great plans for me in Canada and Rev. Ogura of the Methodist Church found my first home with the A. T. Morrow family. Mr. Morrow was the superintendent of Seagrams Distillers in New Westminster and he had a young son, a fine fellow and good company for me. I lived with the Morrows and on February 1922, entered the first grade at Sir Richard McBride School.

Rev. Y. Akagawa of the United Church helped me find my second home with Mrs. Green, an Irish lady who was very understanding. I stayed here until I completed my studies at the Duke of Connaught High School. While at Mrs. Green's I had chores to do in the morning and at night I helped her in the kitchen and dining room as she took in boarders. In those days one had to be Anglo-Saxon to get work in New Westminster. Those of other nationalities and those who came from other towns or provinces had a very difficult time in securing a position in this city.

After spending a year at the University of British Columbia from 1928 to 1929, my future looked a little brighter and I was determined to go ahead with my college education. During summer holidays I used to work on fruit farms or at local lumber mills. From 1928 to 1929, while I was attending university, I got up at four a.m. and worked at Dad's poultry farm, cleaning the chicken house floors for 20,000 chickens. This chore took me 90 minutes. Then I got ready to catch the Varsity Special bus to school in time for the eight-thirty lecture. Three times a week on my way home from university I dropped in at the Japanese United Church Night School and taught English to newly-arrived immigrants for two hours, without remuneration.

Dr. L. S. Klinck, president of the University of British Columbia, negotiated with Dr. Robert Wallace, president of the University of Alberta, to have me transferred to Edmonton where the university fees were $85 a year. University of British Columbia fees were $100. This was a kind gesture to help a poverty-stricken boy. In this transaction I received the special privilege of working in the kitchen, dining and laundry rooms of the university dormitory in exchange for room and board.

During the summer of 1931, I was fortunate enough to work at the C.P.R. Banff Springs Hotel where the King and Queen of Siam (now Thailand) along with their children and accompanying dignitaries were staying. They were returning from New York where the king had had a successful eye operation. They stayed two months in Banff and I was their special night elevator operator.

In 1932, I was the first Japanese Canadian to graduate from the University of Alberta and received a Bachelor of Science in Arts degree.

During the depression years of the thirties I could not earn enough to continue my education and took two and a half years off to work at the English and Wood Co. lumber mills on Vancouver Island.

My strong ambition and earnest desire to study dentistry won over the teaching staff of the University of Oregon Dental School which agreed to help me by deferring payment of tuition fees. They allowed me to take out college text books from the library and use the college dental instruments free of charge. I had to study hard from eight a.m. to seven p.m. six days a week so that two years work could be completed in one. In this way I was able to save quite a bit of money for the senior year. Several of the professors remained after regular classes and helped me with my studies. For my room and board I worked as a janitor at the dental school and at the home of Dr. Herbert Miller, president of the college. In two years and five months I passed all four academic years' examinations — theoretical, practical and clinical requirements and I received the degree of Doctor of Dental Medicine in 1938.

As soon as I returned home from the dental school Dad suffered a heart attack and passed away. Mother said that Dad's ambitions had been carried out satisfactorily and he had asked her to take over the reins of the team work among family and friends.

We opened the dental office in New Westminster and I began my practice. People often remarked that I had a quality of tenderness and was as timid as a lamb but that I was as strong as a horse. In one of the judo tournaments, I defeated two black belts one after the other.

Among the five boys in the family I was the closest to

mother. As there were no girls in our family, I cooked meals, washed clothes, ironed shirts, darned socks and scrubbed floors. She was mother, sister, sweetheart and intimate friend.

When the Second World War came, I tried to enlist in the Canadian Air Force but was rejected because of my racial origin. Just at that time I received a letter from my dear friend who was Minister of Education for Alberta. The letter read as follows:

Dear Paul:

Your letter in reply to ours came a few weeks ago. We are glad to know that you were still carrying on in your regular business even though no one knows just what the future may have in store for any of us. It is a great joy to us to know that you are in good spirits and taking all the upset and confusion without bitterness and hard feeling. We on our part are trying to do the same. As you know we have some thousands of B.C. Japanese in Alberta. During the last few days I have been working on the problems of school accommodation for the 560 children that have come. I plan to go down there to see these boys and girls and try to help them get fitted into their new surroundings. I think the people of the south will take them in and make them feel that over here they will not be objects of suspicion. We have just admitted a young Japanese girl to the normal school to train as a teacher. Of course she is a native Albertan so there can be nothing the matter with her.

If and when you have to leave New Westminster be sure to let us know to what area you have been sent. Should you by any chance come to Alberta, we shall be able to see you since members of our class often go to Lethbridge and other southern towns.

You have never told us that you were married so I assume that you have no wife or children to worry about. I do remember that you spoke several times of your mother. I hope she is well and not too much put about by what is going on.

Please send us a letter soon and in it let us know how you are doing. We are wondering particularly how your mother is standing the change in climate. I hope she is getting accustomed to it and has not suffered too much in the way of dislocation. Please keep in touch with us. We are delighted to know that you have been able to retain the confidence and affection of both your white Canadian friends as well as your Japanese Canadian patients. Some day I hope not too far away we may all be able to live together in peace and understanding.

Kindest yours,

G. Fred McNally

Mother suggested that I work for the Federal Government's project, that is the treatment of tuberculosis patients at the sanatorium to be built in New Denver. In any case, there were no Japanese dentists left at the coast to be sent anywhere. No one wanted to give dental care to infectious tubercular patients and no dentists worked at the Hastings Park tuberculosis quarters when the project was opened at the beginning of the evacuation. A R.C.M.P. representative came to me in New Westminster and begged me to offer my services at Hastings Park. So I received some training at the Tranquille Sanatorium, near Kamloops. In addition, I had some experience at the University Hospital in Edmonton. Mother and I worked hand in hand. We first went to the ghost town of Sandon where about one thousand Japanese evacuees and a few dozen white people lived. We occupied half of an old elementary school building which was no longer in use. When the Roseberry and New Denver projects were opened up for the Japanese evacuees, we moved to our headquarters in New Denver. We were responsible for patients from Roseberry, New Denver, Sandon, Silverton. Nakusp and points down the Arrow Lakes.

In the spring of 1943, Dr. G. Fred McNally paid us a surprise visit. He came with a school inspector from Nelson, B.C. Mother was really delighted to see Dr. McNally. He told us that the Japanese children in southern Alberta were taken care of in a reasonably comfortable manner.

During 1942 to 1949, there was a tremendous amount of study, research and treatment planning in sanitation and nutrition at the Sanatorium. Experts came from Vancouver, Nelson, Trail, and other places to assist in the treatment of the one hundred or more tubercular patients. And after the war different organizations sent out committees to the camps to investigate the work. The Royal Society of Health of England made me a Fellow. And in America, I was honoured by the International College of Nutrition as a Fellow of the College and a Diplomate of the International Board of Applied Nutrition.

In the early 1960's, the Japan International Society was looking for a sister city in Canada and New Westminster was chosen as the first sister city in Canada. Mother was extremely pleased to see a friendly bridge being built. New Westminster sent a seventy-five member concert band as its ambassador to Japan in 1966 composed of high school and university students. As mother could not go because of her age, my wife and I went as interpreters and chaperones. The city council asked me to be their Japanese language interpreter whenever the occasion arose. We were the first Japanese to be invited to the city's New Year's party.

Several years later mother passed away quietly.

The British Columbia's 'Who's Who' of 1981 reports the following: Mrs. Misa Kumagai had three miracles: 1) Destined to death by three medical doctors because of worst kind of arthritis . . . completely cured in five years without medical treatment; 2) Cancer of the throat cured in three years without medical or surgical treatments; 3) Malignant ulcer of left leg calf . . . amputation required from thigh to save her life . . . cured completely without medical or surgical treatments and lived to the ripe old age of ninety-four.

Mother is gone but still lives in me. She is the source of my cheerful feelings and comfort. She will live for a long time as my partner.

Hachiro Miyazawa
Union Organizer

One of several organizations which existed in the early days of Japanese Canadian history was the Labour Union. Almost all of the founders of this organization have passed away except Mr. Hachiro Miyazawa. I visited him at his Vancouver home in 1982 when he was ninety-four years old.

Hachiro Miyazawa was born in Nagano-ken, Japan, in 1888 and came to Canada in 1907 at the age of 19, hoping to earn money to help his family which was facing financial difficulties. When he arrived in Victoria, B.C. he was taken to a Japanese hotel called the Ohzawa Ryokan where he had to undergo a medical examination. It was discovered that he had an eye infection so he had to stay at the Ryokan while he received treatment. He had to pay for both the treatment and the accommodation in advance and stayed about two weeks. When the eye infection cleared, he set off for Vancouver and started to work for the Hastings Sawmill receiving wages of $1.35 per day for ten hours of work. After one year and a half in Vancouver, he moved to Britannia Mines, where his brother was employed. At the mine he received $1.65 per day for ten hours of hard labour, and after one year he was making $2.00 per day. Living conditions here were very primitive and most difficult. It was like living in a dirty stable with many people often sleeping in one bunk and of course there was no privacy. He endured this situation from 1909 to 1917. Later he operated a corner grocery store and a rooming house in Vancouver. Near the store there was a dry cleaning shop which had a dry cleaning plant at Cambie and 5th Avenue. Asked by the shop owner to work at the cleaning plant, Miyazawa accepted and learned the dry cleaning business.

In 1918, he married a lovely, bright young Japanese girl whom he met in Canada. Their first dry cleaning shop was situated in down-town Vancouver on Dunsmuir Street. After two years in his own business, he gave it up and worked for another cleaning shop. Their first son, Ichiro, was born followed by another son, Jiro, and later a daughter, Ruth.

Hachiro Miyazawa was interested in the labour union movement since his early days as a sawmill worker. It was July 1, 1920, when the Japanese Labour Union first met at Alexander Japanese Language School.

"Do you remember who was there at that first meeting?" I asked.

"Mr. Taneji Sada, Mr. Etsu Suzuki, and many sawmill workers from Swanson Bay whose mill was shut down were there," he replied. And with this Mr. Miyazawa eagerly began to read an editorial written by Etsu Suzuki, the editor of *Tairiku Nippo* which dealt with labour movements. Suzuki, a graduate of the Tokyo Waseda University, was an *Asahi* newspaper reporter in Tokyo before he came to Canada. The editorial dealt with problems encountered by oriental Canadians due to the anti-oriental movement.

"What were the reasons for this movement?"

"The employers," Suzuki wrote, "did not object to the Japanese as they were good workers and a source of cheap labour. The group of people who disliked the Japanese were the occidental labourers as it was they who had to compete with the Japanese. The occidental labourers had their own labour union and would not allow the Japanese to join." So the editorial stated that it was necessary for the Japanese to form their own union and later join the Canadian union as a viable group.

At this time the Japanese Canadians did not have the franchise so the politicians did not care about the Japanese. The white union also would not help the Japanese.

"We were just like a football being kicked by both the politicians and the unions from one end of the field to the other," said Miyazawa as he laughed. The Japanese appealed to the Japanese Canadian Association (Nihonjin Kai) and the Consulate of Japan in Vancouver for assistance in combatting the anti-Japanese sentiment but they could not help the labourers. The labourers knew that an organized union such as the Canadian Labour Union had the power to fight for its members but an isolated, unorganized people had no power at all.

"Please tell us how the Japanese Canadian Labour Union was established," I asked.

"Well," Miyazawa replied, "when the First World War ended, Canadian war veterans returned from the war front and discovered that their former positions were filled by the Chinese and Japanese. They were without jobs and so the veterans' resentments towards the orientals were added to the growing anti-Japanese sentiment which was getting stronger and stronger. As we could not get any help from the Nihonjin Kai and the Consulate of Japan, a few of us knew that we must organize our own labour union and so we did. As soon as we began the union, we were regarded as Communists by the members of the community. Japanese Canadians could not understand the difference between the Communists and the labour unions. Even the Consulate of Japan treated us unfavourably."

The leaders of this labour movement, Etsu Suzuki and Takaichi Umezuki, his right hand man had at one time worked together at the *Tairiku Nippo* newspaper office.

Mr. Miyazawa spent many nights at Union meetings and often returned home late. Mrs. Miyazawa worried a great deal and would stay up until his return; there were rumours that people like Hachiro, who would not give up organizing a union, would be beaten up or be killed. Not once did she beg him not to go. Miyazawa commented, "My wife was born to a poor family, and when she was only three years old her mother died; at nine years of age she was sent away to the city of Fukushima about six miles from home to care for her master's child. She attended public school for only two years, so did not have a proper education. However, she was a thoughtful, clever person, a typical Japanese lady, obeying her husband always."

Hachiro Miyazawa's business life was not an easy one as his dry cleaning business partner left him with a debt. When Jiro, their second son was born on December 31st, they had no money to buy fresh milk, so his wife drank canned milk which caused severe diarrhea on New Year's day. Fortunately, through her doctor's care she soon recovered but he remembers this event with sadness. After a time, he succeeded as an independent dry cleaner and built his own cleaning plant with $5,000. While he was enjoying his new found success, the shocking news of the Pacific War came. The family moved to Kamloops in 1942. Miyazawa could not start a business as he was regarded as an enemy alien. Hachiro had to work as a farm labourer. His health broke down and he contacted tuberculosis. He spent two months in the Kamloops Sanatorium and later transferred to the Vancouver Sanatorium where he spent six months before being discharged. They lived in Kamloops for fifteen years before returning to Vancouver. He has since visited Japan several times.

Ichiro, the eldest son, died in an unfortunate accident and the second son, Jiro, became the Secretary-Treasurer of the union at the Kamloops sawmill at an early age. Later Jiro became a union organizer in the Vancouver head office and was sent to Geneva, Switzerland as one of the Canadian delegates to the International Conference of Labour, Management, and Government Officials. He also went to Calcutta, India to help the labour movement in underdeveloped countries of Asia.

Hachiro Miyazawa once suffered a case of pneumonia but is now in good health for a ninety-four-year-old man. He has a keen mind, good eye sight, and hearing. When I asked him his secret of good health, he replied, "Do not ignore your illness. Call the doctor when you are not well. Do not worry about anything. And trust God, just as a child trusts its mother. If you have a heart of thankfulness your complaints will disappear."

The joyful expression of this old gentleman will remain in my heart for a long time.

Peter Eiichi Kuwabara, June 1922
Steveston, B.C.

Segregation of
Japanese Canadian School Children
A Story of Eiichi and Kina Kuwabara C.M.

Japanese Canadians were eager to have their sons and daughters well educated, even though in the British Columbia of the 1920's they were treated as second class citizens — unable to go into such occupations as pharmacy or law, or to hold government office. Government policy of those days was to assimilate people of different racial origins and cultures. So it was natural that Japanese parents sent their children to public schools.

One day in 1924, at the school district of Marpole, B.C. something shocking happened — Japanese children were segregated. Mr. Peter Eiichi Kuwabara, who lived in Marpole and Rev. F. C. Kennedy, the Superintendent of the Anglican Japanese Missions in B.C., immediately worked to solve the problems. The following is the story of the incident as remembered by Kina Kuwabara, the widow of Eiichi Kuwabara.

Due to the conflict between China and Japan, and for other reasons, the Japanese in Canada had to face unpleasant anti-Japanese feelings. However, in our area of Marpole where about twenty-nine Japanese families lived, we had no unhappy incidents until the event of 1924. Our children were happy attending David Lloyd George school. The principal of the school was B. E. Harvey, the school trustees were Dr. Parks, Samuel Churchill, who was also a former reeve, and two others whose names I've forgotten. When our children had health problems the school nurse would send notices or visit us.

For example, Mr. Tanaka who could not read English brought a notice from the school nurse for us to translate. The note said, "Your daughter Kimiko Tanaka has developed whooping cough, so please keep her in the house, away from other children." On another occasion we received a telephone message from the School Trustee, Mr. Samuel Churchill, asking us to advise all Japanese householders to fly the Canadian flag on Dominion Day, July 1, as did all other Canadians. At that time we had a Doshi Kai, a Japanese Association, so we sent the message on to them.

Then one morning in the fall of 1924, suddenly our peaceful existence was shattered. Several Japanese fathers came to our home and excitedly asked to see Mr. Kuwabara. The previous day, which was the first day of school, they took their children to David Lloyd George Public School. Instead of being in the usual class-rooms with all the other children they were gathered together and placed in a separate class-room which was in another building. This action clearly indicated the segregation of Japanese children and the parents were greatly concerned as they did not know what to do. After hearing the details of the previous day Mr. Kuwabara said, "It is a very grave matter. If we do not stop this it may spread to other schools in the greater Vancouver area. We must control ourselves and not take any drastic action. If the policy of the School Board is to segregate the Japanese children from the others I would have been notified by some member of the Board."

As soon as he said this he went out and the fathers returned to their homes. Later, when Mr. Kuwabara returned, he said that Rev. Kennedy was greatly shocked and had promised to meet Mr. Churchill the following day. They went to see Samuel Churchill and Mr. Kuwabara introduced Rev. Kennedy as a missionary who had lived in Japan. Mr. Churchill asked "How many years did you live in Japan, and what do you think of the Japanese people?"

"I lived in Japan for nearly twenty years and found them to be kind, very appreciative and wonderful people," replied Rev. Kennedy.

"Yes, and I know that they are nice people. As I said to Mr. Kuwabara, something must be done about this unhappy situation of the children." added Mr. Churchill.

"The Japanese people are eager to educate their children. To the Japanese Canadians this segregation matter is of great concern. Please do whatever you can to solve this problem. We are going to see Dr. Riggs as well. If we can do anything to avert this problem we must do so. Please help us," begged Rev. Kennedy.

The next day Mr. Kuwabara introduced Rev. Kennedy to Dr. Riggs. The conversation of the previous day was repeated. Rev. Kennedy told Dr. Riggs that he was shocked when he heard of this sad situation and felt that the problem of segregation must be resolved as quickly as possible for if this was not done immediately, the segregation of Japanese children would spread to other public schools in the greater Vancouver area. To this, Dr. Riggs replied that the problem was a grave one and it was not what Japanese Canadians did to white Canadians but rather, it was the result of Japan's actions in China. He agreed that it was not right to segregate the Japanese children and indicated that he would investigate the matter further. Mr. Kuwabara and Rev. Kennedy were advised to meet the school principal the next day. The two men left the doctor's office, their hearts full of hope.

The following day they visited Mr. Bruce Harvey, the principal of David Lloyd George School. Rev. Kennedy repeated much of his previous day's conversations and he asked, "Could you tell us why you are segregating the Japanese children from the others in one crowded class-room and with only one teacher? Is it right for a Christian country such as Canada to act in this way and in a public school system? We visited some of the school trustees and asked them to reconsider the segregation policy. Will you also?"

To this the principal replied, "Our problem is that the Japanese children do not understand English well enough when they enter school. It requires twice as much of the teacher's time to teach them. So we received many complaints from parents of other children because their children return home so late.

Rev. Kennedy then said, "If you stop the segregation, we will start a kindergarten and teach English to the Japanese children from four to six years of age. In this way they will be ready for public school. We will start our kindergarten at St. Augustine's Anglican Church in Marpole where many Japanese children attend Sunday School."

Kina Kuwabara, 1931

Although there would be the problem of financing the project, Rev. Kennedy, because of his strong faith that God would provide, promised to start the kindergarten and he asked the principal to end the segregation. With a firm promise from the principal to end the segregation the two happy gentlemen were about to leave when Mr. Harvey jokingly said, "Mr. Kuwabara, you must have spoken to all the trustees so convincingly that they accepted your suggestions."

"We are going to announce this good news to the Japanese people on September 18th." Mr. Kuwabara replied. "We would like you and the school trustee members to attend this meeting. We will send invitations to you later."

As soon as they were out on the street, Rev. Kennedy said in a loud voice, "Mr. Kuwabara, knock and it shall be opened, neh?" How happy they were as they returned to our home.

On September 18, 1924, it was announced that the segregation of the Japanese children would end and with this notice the Marpole kindergarten was started. The first teacher was Miss Mabel Colton, a very kind teacher, who was assisted by Miss Schetky. Gradually a mother's association was established and Miss Schetky opened her home to the Japanese mothers to learn English. It was a miracle. Peace came back to the Japanese of Marpole. Rev. Kennedy's wonderful work among the Japanese will never be forgotten.

Mr. and Mrs. Kuwabara experienced many other things, but in these few pages we can only share a small amount. Now we will hear more about Mr. Kuwabara.

Peter Eiichi Kuwabara was born in Gifu-ken, Japan and was brought up in a strong Buddhist environment but he was interested in the Christian religion and in learning to speak and write English. At that time the Anglican Church of Canada was undertaking missionary work in the Diocese of mid-Japan which included Gifu-ken. It was about eighty years ago and Christianity was not popular in Japan.

He was sent to school to study the Chinese classics by his father and uncle, but at the same time he was learning about Christianity by visiting the Christian Church and the missionaries there on his way home from the Chinese school. Later he entered Normal school to become a school teacher. While at Normal school he secretly attended the Bible study classes which were conducted by a missionary. He spent some time preaching but was found out by the principal of the school and was forbidden from taking part in further Christian activities. He graduated from the Normal School and was appointed primary school master in a small village. There he was discovered to be a Christian and met with persecution, so he resigned from the school. He visited Bishop Hamilton in Nagoya by whom he had been baptized and confirmed, and told him of his desire to go to Canada. However, it was suggested that he go to Tokyo to study for the ministry. He entered the Tokyo Aoyama Gakuin College and while attending college he received his passport to Canada. After consulting with Bishop Hamilton and Dr. Lee, he came to Canada in 1907. Since there was no work available with the Anglican Church he contracted to work for eight years for the Methodist Japanese Missions. His first mission was at Victoria for a period of two years, followed by two years each in Steveston and Vancouver and then he worked as the Secretary of the Japanese Fishermen's Association. After eight years he left the Methodist Mission work and by this time he was married to his first wife, Hana. They had three sons and were enjoying a happy married life. Unfortunately in 1918, the terrible Spanish flu hit and Hana Kuwabara died in Marpole, a victim of the epidemic. After his first wife's death, Mr. Kuwabara married Kina and they were blessed with a son.

Just before the start of the Pacific War, Peter Eiichi Kuwabara passed away in 1940 at Marpole, leaving behind a great contribution to his family and the Japanese Canadians.

Kina and her family moved to Sandon, B.C. during the war years and later relocated to Montreal where she raised her son Victor. Dr. Edward Kuwabara, the son of Eiichi

Kuwabara and his first wife, Hana, is practicing medicine in Toronto. Kina Kuwabara became a well known teacher of Japanese flower arrangement and in 1977 published a beautiful book titled *Flower and I.* In the same year, she was honoured by the Canadian government for her contributions to Canadian society and made a member of the Order of Canada.

Takuji Maehara
Discoverer of Maehara Delicious Apple

When the Okanagan United Church of Kelowna, B.C. had a meeting entitled, A Dialogue between the Issei and Sansei, *I received an invitation to attend. During this trip I was able to visit some of the early pioneers of Kelowna with Rev. Masao Iwazawa, the minister of the church. Among them were Mr. and Mrs. Takuji Maehara.*

Mr. Maehara was born in 1888 at Hiroshima-ken, Japan. He went to Hawaii when he was seventeen years old and stayed there for two years. Unable to find work in Hawaii, he, along with more than one thousand other Japanese, came to Canada. However, they could not find suitable jobs in British Columbia so Maehara and several others were sent to Maple Creek, Saskatchewan, to work for the C.P.R. by the Nikka Yotatsu' Sha, an employment agency. Unfortunately, when they arrived at Maple Creek there was no work available for them. So they decided to return to British Columbia but they could not afford the train fare. The only thing to do was to walk from Maple Creek to Kelowna, B.C. They slept in the fields or in the woods with just one blanket between them. Hungry and without money, they sometimes received food from the farmers along the side of the highways. They finally arrived at Calgary and then walked to the Rocky Mountains. The construction of a tunnel was going on and they had to go down the steep, dangerous, three-mile hill on a rail truck. On the way down, they saw how steep the hill was for the five engines which were pulling the train up the hill were scarcely moving. It took them forty-two days of mostly walking to reach Kelowna.

Mr. Maehara also remembered an accident that happened at the Rainbow Ranch in the Okanagan Centre. He was on a horse drawn wagon, loaded with apples. One seldom saw automobiles then. On that day, a truck rumbled by and the noise of the truck startled and frightened the horse. It bolted and galloped away leaving the upturned wagon. Fortunately Takuji was not injured but the wagon load of apples was all smashed — a great loss.

Takuji Maehara met his future bride while he was staying at her father's farm in Hawaii. Mrs. Maehara was sent to Japan for her education and in 1920, they were married. At first they settled in Okanagan Centre, B.C. They still remember the kindness shown to them by Mr. and Mrs. Denbei Kobayashi and others while they lived there. At the end of the year 1920, they moved to Kelowna and rented twenty-seven acres of farm land growing tomatoes and onions there. Later they bought an orchard with apples and other fruit trees on a little hill at Rutland near Kelowna. It was on this orchard that he discovered a wonderful new kind of apple. I did not know that one type of red delicious apples was originated at the Maehara's twenty-three acre orchard in 1956.

One autumn day, Takuji found some brilliant red apples on a lower branch of a green apple tree. This branch did not get enough sun and yet the apples were a beautiful red colour. He picked one and tasted it. It was delicious! He reported this discovery to the Dominion Experimental Farm in Summerland, B.C. Soon an official agriculturalist came to the farm, tasted this unusually beautiful apple and said, "Oh, this is very good Maehara. Delicious." This is how the new kind of Maehara Delicious apple became known throughout North America. Mr. Maehara busily laboured to increase production of this new variety of Delicious apples. Within ten years he had thirty trees from this one tree and was able to send many young plants to many parts of North

America including the University of California and a university in Idaho, U.S.A., as well as to other experimental stations.

Mr. and Mrs. Maehara are blessed with six children, fourteen grandchildren, and six great grandchildren. In his lifetime, Takuji recalled there had been many wars— the China-Japan war, the Russia-Japan war, the First World War and the Second World War. But when I spoke to him, he was at 94 years of age, enjoying a life without strife, peaceful and content with his loving wife.

Rokusuke Maeda
Barber on a Bicycle

It so happened on a winter day in 1946, when I was a pastor at the Japanese Anglican Mission in Coaldale, Alberta that I was pedalling my bike along the country road of Turin, some 35 miles north-east of Coaldale. Due to a sudden chinook wind which melted the snow, the gumbo was making it impossible for me to keep pedalling. While I wondered what to do, an automobile came by driven skillfully by a lovely young lady. It was Miss Jessie Maeda, the future bride of Mr. T. S. Suzuki (I was later to perform the marriage ceremony for them). Miss Maeda kindly gave me a ride and took me to her home in a farm near the town of Turin, Alberta. Thus we all became good friends.

The story of Mr. Maeda is very interesting and unique. This is the article written by Mrs. Jessie Maeda Suzuki.

My father, Rokusuke Maeda, was born in Okayama Japan in 1888. He came to Canada in 1907 to work with the C.P.R. work gang. On one occasion he and two companions left their jobs at a work camp at Glacier and headed for the "Rich land of Texas", in the dead of night. They crossed the border only to be caught and sent back to Canada. They soon learned that their escape from Glacier saved their lives. The night they left, a snow slide buried their camp and workers.

Rokusuke Maeda and associate
Mikizo Nishiguchi, New Westminster, 1911

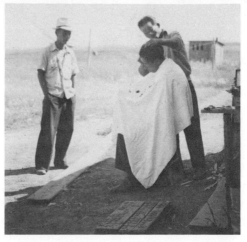

Rokusuke Maeda with hand clippers on
Sugar beet farm in Turin, Alberta,
Aug 1942. Furoba in background.

He worked at numerous jobs suffering discrimination from the whites as did other colored immigrants. He finally settled down to a job in a sawmill near New Westminster. One day while waiting for his turn in a barber shop, he decided to become a barber. He went regularly to this shop every weekend for a neck trim or a shave. The barber thought he was overly fastidious about his grooming. He would go on busy Saturdays when the shop was filled and he would wait his turn. He observed how the barber held his comb, used the scissors and how he stropped the razor, etc. He would return to the sawmill bunk house and practice on his fellow employees. Finally, after several years he and a friend, Mr. Nishiguchi opened up their barbershop in New Westminster. While there he met the Chinese Elder from Ladner Chinatown who persuaded him to move to Ladner. In 1912 when Sun Yat Sen came into power in China the Chinese men were allowed to cut off their queues. The queues had signified servitude to the previous government. The Chinese were overjoyed.

The Elder advised my father to set aside a special time for the men and to treat each haircut with the utmost reverence. The pigtail was cut, placed on a clean towel and presented to its owner. An empty cigar box was placed on a table near the door and each man would drop in money wrapped in red paper. They were very generous and my father had never seen so much money in all his life. The following year he sent for my mother from Japan. In 1921 he built a home and barber shop and barbered there until the evacuation in 1942. They raised seven children.

He became known as "the barber on the bicycle." He would take his equipment in a suitcase and ride out to service shut-ins and invalids. He was also known to give free haircuts to welfare recipients.

His hobby was growing prize chrysanthemums, many of which adorned the altars of local churches and other social functions. He was also an avid duck hunter and interested himself in the different species of ducks. He carved wooden decoys and painted them himself. Today his decoys are collectors' items and are frequently displayed in the sport shows at the Pacific National Exhibition. There is a picture of his barberhop and a brief write-up about him at the Ladner Museum.

In 1942, he and his family relocated to Turin, Alberta to work in the sugarbeets. He began to cut hair for his friends and neighbours with hand clippers as there was no electricity. He would not take money but was reimbursed with various products such as milk, eggs, chickens, ham, etc. and many favours but most of all friendship that he appreciated very much.

Then a businessman in Turin town made space for my father in his coffee shop to set up barbering. As he needed a licence he went to Lethbridge and took a barber's exam. He passed and received his licence. That was the proudest moment of his life.

His pastime in Alberta was raising chickens. When he first started out he combed the neighboring farms for fertilized chicken eggs. He would inspect each egg by kerosene lamp light and he would select the ones that would hatch. The farmers in the district would take all their eggs to the Lethbridge hatchery where they would be put into incubators. The farmers would get twenty-five cents a dozen and five cents for each egg that hatched. When word got around about my father selecting hatching eggs he became known as "the crazy Jap on Mitchell's farm". However, after 21 days under brooding hens each batch of 13 eggs hatched to the astonishment of the townspeople. Before coming to Canada my father had attended a chicken school in Nagoya.

In 1950 he and his family returned to B.C. and settled in Richmond where he continued to barber until his retirement. Both my mother and father wished to be buried in the Ladner Cemetery among their many friends of the community where they spent the happiest years of their lives.

Kiyosuke Iwabuchi
Founder of I & S Produce Limited

If you ever visit Edmonton, Alberta you will find a very large vegetable and grocery wholesale establishment near the C.N.R. station which covers almost a whole block.

It bears the name of I & S Produce Limited. I & S stands for Iwabuchi and Sons. The founders of this big establishment are the late Mr. Kiyosuke Iwabuchi, his wife, Kiyoshi, and their sons William K., Jack, and Robert. In 1982 there were 125 people both occidental and Japanese Canadians working there. I was surprised to find the offices completely computerized. In the plant huge automatic potato chip and salad making machines are working. They buy fruit, vegetables and groceries from all over the world and sell them mostly to hospitals, restaurants and all kinds of institutions such as to the Food Floors of the Woodwards store.

Kiyosuke Iwabuchi was born in Miyagi-ken, Japan in 1880. He immigrated to Canada in 1908 to work on the construction of the C.P.R.'s trans-Canada line. In 1919, he married Kiyoshi in Japan and returned to Canada the same year. The first place he worked was at Fort McLeod, Alberta in the C.P.R. shop. After that he, his wife and first child Kathleen moved to Raymond, Alberta, where he farmed for a short while on a farm he bought, and grew potatoes. Their second daughter was born in Raymond.

Mr. Iwabuchi had a close friend, Mr. Miyauchi, who lived in Brandon, Manitoba. Persuaded by Mr. Miyauchi, the Iwabuchi family moved to Brandon in 1921 and they lived there for 18 years. Here he did market gardening in the summer and worked with the C.P.R. during winter. Life was hard. During these years eight more children were born making ten — seven daughters and three sons. For two consecutive years a big flood wiped out their crops and they lost everything.

"As we did not have enough wood to burn for cooking, we dried the stems and roots of cabbages for fuel," Mrs.

Iwabuchi recalled. "We did not have enough food to eat, nor enough clothing to wear. We were in a desperate situation. Then one day Dr. and Mrs. Norman, missionaries from Japan, came to visit us. These Methodist missionaries taught us about the love of God. Our harsh life continued and one day in 1942, when I could not endure the hardship any longer, I sat all alone weeping loudly. Suddenly I found myself shouting, 'The Spirit of God lifts us up.' For the first time in my life my heart was filled with joy and peace. And from that day, my hope has never since been lost." She was speaking with a radiant face, at eighty-eight years of age.

While they were in Brandon, Kiyosuke Iwabuchi saw a vision of Christ in a dream showing him a map and telling him to go to a certain spot in a Southern Alberta town with a farm ranch around it. Like Abraham in ancient Israel, Kiyosuke followed the guidance of God, who appeared in a dream. His great ambition had always been to return to Japan, but following the dream and leaving his family behind in Brandon, he wandered around Southern Alberta in search of the promised place. He first settled at Barnwell, Alberta. Here he cultivated and grew cabbages and other vegetables, and also worked as a sugar beet labourer. However after a time, convinced that Taber, Alberta, not Barnwell was the promised place he returned to Brandon. The family moved to Taber in the spring of 1939.

Mr. W. S. Hall, an earnest Christian and the manager of Broder Canning Co., helped the Iwabuchi family to start their farming venture. It was not an easy task to begin farming in a new location. The first summer Bill, Jack, and Bobby lived in farmer Green's granary. In the fall of that same year they bought a house on the north east edge of the town of Taber, adding a greenhouse and a large cellar close by. The children went to school and helped in the farm work after school was over. They bought a thirty-acre farm growing ten acres each of tomatoes, peas and various other vegetables. They harvested a good crop that year and thus began the Iwabuchi success story, a story that touches the lives of three sons and seven daughters, Kathleen, Helen, Betty, Dorothy,

Vera, Verna, Bill, Jack, Bobby, and Joyce. Some years later they purchased a farm in Vauxhall, where they grew potatoes. Vauxhall became one of the largest potato growing districts in Canada.

As their farming enterprise grew, their Christian faith also grew and deepened and most of the children after graduating from high school attended Bible Schools in Saskatchewan. Dorothy became a Christian missionary and went to Japan to the city of Beppu. She is now married and is the mother of two sons.

In Taber, they built a church with the help of Mr. Hall, naming it Taber Gospel Hall. It was a means of serving many Japanese Canadian evacuees, as well as other local people. The Iwabuchi house became the centre of Christian missionary evangelistic work. Mr. and Mrs. C. Wilkinson, English missionaries who came to Canada from Japan due to the Second World War, lived with them for two years.

One particularly noteworthy service performed by Mr. Iwabuchi was in the area of Japanese immigration to Canada. In his eagerness to facilitate and assist in the matter, he travelled to Ottawa to see the Japanese ambassador and Canadian officials. He also went to Japan visiting the Minister of Foreign Affairs, urging him to negotiate the immigration question with the Canadian government. Eventually the door for Japanese immigrants opened again in 1965.

In recognition of his contributions, the Japanese government awarded him with a silver medal and a special citation from Prince Takamatsu, who is the President of the 'All Japan Agricultural Association.' In 1967, Mr. and Mrs. Iwabuchi met their Imperial Highnesses, Prince and Princess Takamatsu of Japan when they opened the Lethbridge Centennial Nikka Yuko Garden.

In 1969, Mr. and Mrs. Iwabuchi celebrated their golden wedding anniversary, a happy occasion, with all their children and grand-children. Only Dorothy Doi, who lives in Japan could not come.

Kiyosuke Iwabuchi's colourful and wonderful life here on earth came to an end in Edmonton in 1970. I was privileged to deliver the eulogy at the funeral service — a few words to remember and honour one of our outstanding Japanese Canadian pioneers.

Tome Ueda
Picture Bride

At the turn of the century most Japanese immigrants in Canada were young men whose ambition was to accumulate as much money as possible and then return to their native country to establish their family lives. However, they soon discovered that the material gain which they sought was not so easy to obtain. As the years flew by these men were obliged to remain in Canada and search for potential wives. But because of the anti-Japanese sentiment of the day, it was almost impossible for a Japanese man to marry a white Canadian woman and thus the practice of the 'picture bride marriage' arose. It involved exchanging photographs with a young, eligible woman in Japan and arranging for her passage to Canada.

In April, 1982, while visiting the Hinode Japanese Canadian Senior Citizens' Home in Kelowna, B.C., I caught a glimpse of life as a picture bride through my conversation with Mrs. Tome Ueda. Then ninety-four years old, Tome Ueda came to Canada in 1888 at the age of twenty from her birthplace, Fukuoka-ken, in order to marry Mr. Nobujiro Ueda. Her story of hardship and suffering exemplifies that of many other Japanese women who came to this country with similar dreams and under similar circumstances.

"I came to Canada as a 'picture bride'," stated Mrs. Ueda. "And when I came to Kelowna I was greatly shocked. I almost fainted."

"Why were you so shocked?" I asked.

"I came to Canada with a great dream — to live in a lovely home with lots of nice food to eat. In those days in Japan we were told that America — including Canada — was a very rich country where people were wealthy. I only imagined a happy, peaceful, easy life. But when I found there was not even a house to live in I was shocked."

"What? Not even a house to live in? Then what did you do?"

"We had to live in a tent which was in the farm field, and it was a very small one. I could not even enter it upright, so I had to bend my body."

"How about a bed?"

"An old, wretched wooden bed. You have probably never seen such a bed, not even among the poorest people in Japan."

"What about food? Did you have enough to eat?"

"Yes, we had enough rice, but not enough okazu (side dishes). There were no green vegetables, only onions and potatoes. We bought some iriko (dried fish) but not much more."

"Did you have a Japanese store in Kelowna?"

"Yes, there was Mr. K. Iwashita's store, but the old store was burnt down a year before I came and they were building a new one. They did not have much of anything, so we had to eat potatoes and onions every day."

Mr. Ueda was working with his friends, Mr. and Mrs. Nakatsubo. This couple lived in a one room shack built with rough lumber. The roof was just one side. Before the cold winter arrived the newly wed Uedas built the same kind of shack for themselves. And while Mrs. Nakatsubo cooked the meals for both couples, Mrs. Ueda had to work in the field with the men.

"You must have found the life in your early days in Canada very, very hard." I remarked.

"Yes. None of the younger generation understands or believes what a hard life we old pioneers had to go through."

"Were there many Japanese here when you arrived?"

"Not very many. There were only five other women besides me, and of these women I am the only one still living."

In 1926 Mrs. Ueda's husband passed away at the age of

forty-two. Thus Mrs. Tome Ueda became a widow at age thirty-eight with six children to raise, the oldest of whom was only eleven years old. The fatherless family had neither a house nor money, as Mr. Ueda had unfortunately spent his money on gambling. The task of feeding, clothing and caring for six small children in a foreign land was a heavy responsibility for a young woman like Tome. Her mother and older brother urged her to return to Japan with her children, but she dared not do so, as she had come to Canada in the first place in opposition to her family's wishes.

With the help of Mr. Iwashita she rented some farm land and grew tomatoes and onions, so that she and her children could survive. Fortunately, Mrs. Ueda's children were healthy and grew up without any major problems.

Today Tome Ueda is enjoying her retirement years with two sons and four daughters all married, fifteen grandchildren, and twelve great grandchildren.

"Do you remember any old timers from your early days in Canada?" I asked.

"Yes, I still remember Mr. and Mrs. Terai, Mr. and Mrs. Yamamoto and Mr. and Mrs Nakatsubo. But they have all gone, and I'm the only one still living . . ."

"Do you remember a particularly happy occasion?"

"Yes, I was very happy when my last daughter married. I sent all my daughters off with a bedroom suite and a sewing machine to begin their married lives. I felt so happy as I finished my task as a mother by giving my last daughter away in marriage."

Mrs. Ueda seemed very well at the age of ninety-four yet I discovered that she has heart trouble and a pacemaker was placed in her chest six years ago.

Genroku Nakamura
Who Cleared Forests

I went to visit eighty-two year old Mrs. Matsu Furukawa of Vancouver whose father, the late Mr. Genroku Nakamura actually cleared forests in Vancouver, helping to create Trout Lake, the University of B.C. Campus, Point Grey, Burnaby and the city as we now know it. It is not such a long time ago that this city was a wilderness.

"My father was born in Fukui-ken, Japan, in 1863 (Keio, 1st year)." Mrs. Furukawa said. "He came to Canada alone leaving his wife (my mother), my older brother and myself. First he went to Hawaii but he changed his plans and came to Canada. I do not know whether he planned to come to Canada from the beginning or not."

"Do you know why he left Japan — even leaving his family there?" I asked.

"Well, I think he needed money to establish a farm implement factory. He had invented a method of fumigating mulberry trees on which silk worms feed. Until he came to Canada he had been a teacher at an agricultural school. He called us to Canada in 1910."

"What did he do after he arrived here?"

"At first he could not understand English. He sought the help of his friend, Mr. Tomoda, who had an office on the second floor over Mr. Saegusa's shoe shop in 400 block Powell Street."

Gradually he began his own business. First, he contracted to cut cedar logs for a shingle mill at Capilano, North Vancouver. He bought this business from Mr. Kato together with a donkey machine which was costly. He was in debt to the machine company so the donkey was taken away from him and he could not carry on.

After the Capilano project ended, he contracted to clear the forest in the Trout Lake area in Vancouver. He hired a number of workers and that year, 1910, he called his family from Japan. While they were clearing in what is now the lovely Trout Lake Park, they found a stream. They formed a dyke to make a lake and cleared the west side of the lake, leaving the east side a thick forest. On the west side, they set up tents, making a camping ground that included a Japanese bath house. In the summer of that year a forest fire broke out in the area and the workers went to fight the fire.

Mrs. Furukawa continued her story with a happy recollection. "In the fall we had a lot of rain and the stream flooded. I was ten years old and when I woke up one morning I found the tent had about two feet of water in it and a big salmon was swimming around." Mrs. Furukawa smiled as she remembered how excited she was.

After finishing the Trout Lake project, her father contracted the clearing of the Point Grey district, around Tenth Avenue and Crown Street where a Roman Catholic church and school now stand. He then moved on to Burnaby North, around Boundary Road.

While her father was clearing land and fighting forest fires, young Miss Nakamura attended the Japanese Kokumin Gakko at Alexander Street, the first principal of the school being Mr. Takata and the second, Mr. Tashiro.

Mr. Nakamura owned two lots at Marine Drive and four acres in Burnaby. He sold some of his property and invested the money in property at Fort George, B.C. (now Prince George). Unfortunately for so many, the depression caused much suffering and Mr. Nakamura who was once a wealthy person was among those whose wealth was lost.

But while he was wealthy, he had brought many rare flowers and bonsai (dwarf trees) from Japan. He opened a flower shop on Powell Street and the family's three-acre farm in Richmond was devoted to the cultivation of about five hundred species of Japanese irises.

Genroku Nakamura died in 1921.

Yoshimitsu Akagawa
Missionary and Pastor

*It was not easy to pick which story to tell of the many pioneer
Christian ministers in Canada. In 1930, when the famous Dr.
Toyohiko Kagawa and his secretary Rev. Shiro Kuroda, visited
Canada, a photograph was taken which included eleven
Japanese ministers. I am the only person in that photograph still
living.*

*Yoshimitsu Akagawa was my uncle-in-law and he influ-
enced my entry into the ministry. His biography, 'My Life is My
Message: The Akagawa Story' was written by his faithful friend
and journalist, T. H. Mayeda. Those who wish to obtain the
book may write to Mr. Mayeda at 5 Massey Square, Toronto,
Ontario. The main text is in Japanese with each chapter sum-
marized in English. The following is taken from Mr. Mayeda's
book.*

Yoshimitsu Akagawa was born on July 13, 1880 in Toku-
shima, Japan. Little is known about his early life, as he did
not talk about himself much. He was of samurai descent. His
father was an expert teacher of kendo. Yoshimitsu however,
did not follow the family martial arts tradition, becoming
instead an ardent follower of Christ. He studied theology at
Aoyama Gakuin University in Tokyo.

After graduating from university he became the assistant minister of Ginza Methodist Church in Tokyo. Two
years later he set out for the United States of America,
where he intended to do postgraduate study at a theological
college in Madison, New Jersey. This plan, however, gave
way to other developments and he never reached his original
destination.

Rev. Akagawa arrived in Seattle, Washington in the
summer of 1910 and immediately began helping the
Japanese church there. During this time, Dr. Hartwell of the
Oriental Mission of the British Columbia Conference asked
Rev. Akagawa to assist in church work in the Japanese com-

Japanese Canadian clergy gathering on the occasion of the visit of Dr. Toyohiko Kagawa. (Back L. to R.) Jun Kabayama, United Church; Bernard F. Oana, Anglican; Yutaka Ogura, U.C.; Gordon Goichi Nakayama, U.C.; Kunichi Nomoto, U.C.; Kosaburo Shimizu, U.C.; Tadashi Matsumoto, Ang. (Front L. to R.) Zengo Higashi, Gospel; Yoshinosuke Yoshioka, U.C.; Toyohiko Kagawa; Yoshimitsu Akagawa, munity of the New Westminster district. He was faced with a difficult decision. He had promised the superintendent of the church mission in Japan that after a few years of study abroad he would return to work in the mission field in Japan. Now Dr. Hartwell was presenting an urgent appeal for help in Canada. Rev. Akagawa agreed to stay for a short time in New Westminster before travelling to New Jersey. That short time stretched into over forty years of faithful service to the Japanese community in Canada.

It was a fall night in 1910 when Rev. Akagawa arrived in Vancouver from Seattle on the Great Northern Train. Nobody met him at the station. The next morning he went to Sapperton Church and his ministry in Canada began.

The church was a remodelled building that used to be a Chinese boarding house; meetings were held downstairs and there was a dormitory upstairs. Here he met a young Columbian College student, Kozo Shimotakahara (whose story is elsewhere in this collection) and the two became close and lifelong friends.

The first Bible study meeting was held at Sapperton Church with only one young man in attendance. On the same day a worship service was held in the downtown meeting place by the Fraser River, called "Ukimido" or "Floating Pavillion". Some time later the congregation moved into one half of the Chinese Mission building and this downtown church became headquarters for the Akagawa ministry in New Westminster.

Rev. Akagawa wrote in his memoirs; "There is no church record, nor are there regular meetings, but I love the location with the great Fraser River flowing by and in the far distance one can see high mountains. There is a good community in the district with many people working at the nearby sawmills. My mission is to spread the gospel. There are abundant opportunities for God's work.

After a year and a half at Sapperton Church, Rev. Akagawa went to Toronto, Ontario and he enrolled at Victoria College in the University of Toronto. He took a full course of theology and optional subjects for two years.

Yoshimitsu Akagawa, Tokyo

After completing his two-year theology course, he was preparing to return to Japan as he had promised. Also he wanted to see his father whom he had not visited since his youth. But just about this time he received news that his father had passed away. Because of this sad event, as well as the arrival of an invitation from Dr. Osterhout to work in B.C., he decided to return to new Westminster.

In January of 1915, Rev. Akagawa married Miss Yasuo Ohno, a graduate nurse trained at Kyoto Medical College. Mrs. Akagawa was a good wife and tireless helper to her husband.

In 1916, he became an ordained minister of the Methodist church. Part of his time was spent on mission trips to Cumberland on Vancouver Island.

During the last half of his second New Westminster period, the Japanese community faced some difficult times, for World War I was in progress. Immigration was restricted, and anti-Japanese sentiment ran high. The Vancouver and Steveston communities experienced the most serious troubles, and the church ministers all tried hard to solve their social difficulties. When the Vancouver minister resigned, Reverend Akagawa was asked to take over. Although he was reluctant to move into such a troubled area, he felt compelled to go.

In June 1917 he took over the Vancouver charge, and for about a year he looked after both Vancouver and New Westminster until his successor in New Westminster was found. During the next seven years, Reverend and Mrs. Akagawa worked diligently in Vancouver. He continued to publish the church paper *Hokko (The Northern Light);* tried to make the church self-supporting; re-opened the meeting place and the night school in the Fairview district; set up a special hospital at Strathcona Public School for Japanese patients when the Spanish flu struck Vancouver in 1918, built a large brick gymnasium next to the church for the growing number of young people; put more emphasis on the English-language night school for newcomers from Japan; started a church women's group under the leadership of Mrs.

Yasuno Akagawa

Akagawa; made pioneering trips to various parts of British Columbia, founded the Ocean Falls Mission and the Okanagan Valley Mission, and also organized a Japanese church conference to plan for future work; helped and guided people with various family problems, for instance regarding Canadian-born children who were called back to Canada after being educated in Japan or concerning picture brides who came from Japan. It was about this time that the Japanese in Canada began thinking seriously of staying in Canada rather than returning to Japan.

Between 1924 to 1934, Reverend Akagawa established church missions in the Fraser Valley farming districts of Pitt Meadows, Hammond, Haney, Mission City, Strawberry Hill, Surrey, and many other small villages. Sunday schools, C.G.I.T., young people's groups, kindergartens and women's groups were started all over the countryside.

In 1926, with a generous contribution from Mr. Shigesaburo Ubukata of Toronto, a few acres of farm land were purchased in Burquitlum, a few miles east of New Westminster. Here, with the help of his followers Reverend Akagawa tried to set up a self-supporting Christian Centre for the needy, called Beulah Home. From here he carried on his ministry in New Westminster and the farming districts of the Fraser Valley.

His most outstanding achievement was the "hundred souls campaign". Around 1930 numerous evangelistic meetings were held at various locations with the help of church members and ministers in the area. It was during this time, for example, that at one service in Mission City over fifty persons received baptism.

In May of 1934 Reverend Akagawa took a trip to Japan. His stay was cut short when Mrs. Akagawa fell ill, and he returned to Canada in July.

Reverend Akagawa left the New Westminster Church in the latter part of 1934 to concentrate his efforts in the Fraser Valley.

The Fraser Valley Japanese United Church was established in 1934. An old abandoned church building in Hammond was repaired by church members and the dedication service of this new Maple Ridge Church was held on October 28, 1934.

In Haney the church meetings were continued at the Japanese Farmers' Community Hall. The Corner Mission Sunday School, an international non-denominational school which was started in 1917 by the Hall family and Mr. Y. Yamaga, also flourished.

In Mission City, a Sunday school was started in 1938 and the new church building was started in 1941 by the enthusiasm of the people in this area. In spite of a great deal of confusion and uncertainty because of the Pacific War, the job was completed in 1942. The dedication service of the new church, however, never took place, for the Japanese had to leave the district.

When the war broke out in December of 1941, Reverend Akagawa immediately set out to visit each home, giving the people advice and encouragement. He wrote in his diary that attendance gradually decreased but the spirit remained quite high. His last words to his congregation during the evacuation were to act and live courageously as good Christians no matter where they were.

In May of 1942 Reverend Akagawa was assigned to Manitoba. The Akagawas left Beulah Home in their old car on June 11, 1942. They crossed the Rocky Mountains and the prairie provinces and reached Morris, Manitoba, on June 24, 1942 after a fourteen-day motor trip.

In Manitoba, Reverend Akagawa immediately started out to visit his people, who were scattered around the sugar beet area of Southern Manitoba. He averaged 1,400 miles a month. Using small country churches, community halls, school rooms and farm houses he met with the hundred or so Christians among the 1,000 Japanese in the area.

The war ended August 15, 1945. As part of the government's resettlement programme, the army camp at Transcona, just outside Winnipeg, was used as a relocation centre for the Japanese evacuees. Reverend and Mrs.

Akagawa were active at the Transcona Manning Centre, helping people and holding church meetings.

By this time many of the sugar beet workers had moved into the city. The Manitoba Japanese United Church was organized in Winnipeg. Never one to stay still, Reverend Akagawa started Christian gatherings in Fort William (now part of Thunder Bay).

Forty years of devoted ministry in Canada were acknowledged in October of 1949, when the Manitoba congregation honoured Reverend and Mrs. Akagawa at a special gathering.

In May, 1950 during the Manitoba Flood, the Akagawa home, now located on Midwinter Avenue in the Elmwood district, was flooded when the Red River overflowed its banks. Later that year, in a bad storm a maple tree fell on the kitchen roof. Also during this summer Reverend Akagawa became ill. On the last Sunday of 1950 he announced his retirement from active service; nevertheless, he continued to work until the end of June, 1951.

Mrs. Yasuno Akagawa passed away suddenly on April 19, 1955, stricken with a fatal heart attack. After his wife's death, Reverend Akagawa's health continued to deteriorate. Totally exhausted from a lifetime of hard work, his physical and mental resources weakened. At seventy-six years of age, he passed away peacefully on October 21, 1956.

The funeral was held in Young Street United Church in Winnipeg. Many friends wrote about their great friend and minister. His faithful follower Rev. Kosaburo Shimizu wrote in his tribute to him: Reverend Akagawa was a good pastor. He visited his people and befriended them. He loved his people and spared no time or effort in offering necessary services to them. He was also concerned with the welfare of the Japanese Community as a whole. He assisted his people in their process of assimilation to the Canadian life.

Reverend Yoshimitsu Akagawa and Mrs. Yasuno Akagawa rest in Elmwood Cemetery near the Red River in Winnipeg. On their tombstone is the inscription: My Life is My Message.

Koryo Tanaka
Golfer

"Did you know that there's a Japanese Canadian golfer who made two aces on one round?" a friend of mine asked me one day.

"No," I replied. "Who is he and where and when did this happen?"

"He's Koryo Tanaka. He lives in Toronto now and is ninety years old. Mr. Tanaka is one of my best friends and I've known him since the Second World War days in Slocan, B.C. He made this rare achievement of two holes in a single round at Langara Golf Course in Vancouver on March 6th, 1927."

I asked my friend to explain to me how Mr. Tanaka performed such an almost miraculous feat. In response to my request he sent me an old magazine, 'The American Golfer' (May, 1927). I would like to quote sections from the article on Mr. Tanaka, a remarkable sportsman.

Granted that a hole in one is a matter of pure accident, a friendly nod from Lady Luck, and nothing more; granted that even the greatest players would not care to back themselves at their own odds to sink a tee shot, there still remains a certain soul-stirring throb to the achievement, even for the most stolid and unemotional. There, for once if never again, is the achievement of perfection, and it's a g-r-a-n-d and g-l-o-r-i-o-u-s feeling! The list of those who have achieved this distinction is a long one, and it is growing. There are those who have soared to the heights more than once, some of them several times. But we have here to record a case which must be recorded. It is an almost incredible achievement of two holes in a single round. This performance belongs to Mr. K. Tanaka, a bookseller of Vancouver, B.C., and was achieved on the sixth day of March over the Langara Link, a course built and maintained by the Canadian Pacific Railway at Vancouver.

As companions in the round, were his friends, T. Ode, S. Isogai and J. T. Niimi, all prominent businessmen in Vancouver's Japanese business colony. Besides these men, there were E. S. McCadden, manager of the course, and several other spectators who had watched the match from the start to observe Mr. Tanaka try out some theories which he had been propounding. And thereby hangs a yarn from which the editor of *The American Golfer* may properly preen himself with a reasonable pride. But Mr. Tanaka speaks excellent English, so suppose we allow him to tell the story in his own way.

"Yes, I give *The American Golfer* the credit for my performance of making two holes in one single round of the course. Here is why it happened. I took up golf nearly two years ago, and am still in the duffer class, but I am very fond of the game. Because of my business I get little opportunity to play, no more than once a week, but even at that I find it of great benefit to me in that it keeps me in good physical condition."

"Under the circumstances, it was rather to be expected, I suppose, that I would be a poor player, and I was. I could hit the ball, but I had no idea where it would go when I did. One time it was an artistic slice that left me deep in the rough to the right of the fairway; another time it would be a bad hook that left me equally as bad off in the rough to the left. And the number of balls I lost! Say, my friends got to where they asked me how many balls I needed to get around, instead of what my score was in strokes. It was enough reckoned on either basis.

"But the more I played the more determined I became to make the very most of the limited time I had for the game. I read every book I could find and asked questions, to any of those whom I met who appeared to play a pretty good game. But still my trouble stayed with me. One day it would be slicing, and another hooking, but it was one or the other every time I went to the course.

"Then my attention was called to an article in *The American Golfer.* I read it over and over several times and it seemed to fit my case nicely. I took out a club and began to swing it as the article directed to help to correct my troubles.

Later issues of this magazine, I found, contained other articles of a similar nature devoted to pointing out the causes for
different problems, and the proper methods for correcting
them. I studied all of them carefully. Furthermore, in my
home I took my club and tried out the correct methods of
swinging as explained in these articles. I kept this up day
after day, believing that at last, I was beginning to get going
along the right course.

"Well, I kept patiently at this study and practise until I
felt pretty sure that I had made some real headway from this
indoor play, and then I announced to some of my friends
that I was about ready to go out and show them I had at last
learned something about controlling the ball when I hit it. I
don't need to tell you that I was very greatly pleased, when I
found on my first few trials on the course that my study and
practise had turned the trick. When I hit the ball it travelled
straight in the direction for which I was aiming, and then I
knew that I was on my way.

"I don't mean to say that my lessons and practise have
developed me from a rank dub to the champion class — far
from it. I have still a long way to go. Neither can I say that the
lessons actually taught me how to make a hole in one. But
they did teach me how to hit the ball in the direction desired,
and I should never have made even one hole-in-one as long
as I had no idea where the ball was going. I am pleased to find
that I am now heading in the right direction, and that with
further practise, my game ought to improve still more.
Naturally I want to play as well as I can."

The first of the two 'aces' scored by Mr. Tanaka came
at the fifth hole, which measures 185 yards. The ball landed
on a slope fronting the green and rolled straight into the cup.
The second 'ace' was made at the sixteenth hole and the circumstances were decidedly thrilling. In this case, the ball
landed on the putting green and rolled forward toward the
hole. The players in the match did not dare to hope that
another tee shot was to be holed during the round, but there
was the ball rolling straight for the cup, and to the cup it
went. But the flagstick was in the position and the ball rolled

up against it and stopped on the very edge of the cup. As the players rushed excitedly forward there was much speculation as to what was to be done. No one was quite sure just what the rule was in such matters. However fortune intervened to save them from their predicament. Quite a stiff wind was blowing at that moment, and just as the party reached the green a gust of wind caused the flagstick to lurch slightly away from the ball, thereby widening the space between to allow the ball to drop in the cup.

What an unforgettable thrill Koryo Tanaka and his friends must have experienced that day. I got in touch with two of his friends, Mr. and Mrs. Toragoro Niimi of Richmond, B.C., who assured me that the event had indeed taken place and spoke fondly about it.

Mr. Tanaka's achievement was reported by a special telegram of the news service to all the principal cities of the world and was described in the sports pages of various newspapers on March 8th, 1927. There had been no previous record of "two aces in one round" in Canada, so Mr. Tanaka must have set a major record in the world of golf.

Fortunately, Mr. Niimi is still alive and in good health, but both Mr. Takejiro Ode and Mr. Sotaro Isogai, Mr. Tanaka's other old golfing buddies, have passed away. It would have been wonderful if they could all meet again to recollect the happy fellowship of their youth.

Ed's note: Mr. Tanaka advises that the No. 5 hole was 115 yds. and the No. 16 hole was 235 yds.

Karen, Andrew Shoji, Henry
Mrs. Kimiko Shimizu, Mrs. Grace Sakamoto
Mr. Shotaro Shimizu

Mr. and Mrs. Shotaro Shimizu
A Couple Who Loved Trees

My dear friend, Shotaro Shimizu, died shortly after I interviewed him for this book. He and his wife contributed greatly not only to the welfare of the Japanese, but to the larger Canadian community wherever they lived.

Shotaro Shimizu was born in Nara-ken, Japan near the famous Shinto shrine Kashiwasa in 1886. Immediately after graduating from Sunebi High School in 1909 he came to Seattle, Washington.

"Had you any special purpose in coming to North America?" I asked him.

"Yes, I had two hopes or purposes. One was to become a good American citizen and the other was to leave my offspring here. I hoped they would contribute to world peace in some way."

"Those are worthy objectives," I commented. "And why did you come to Canada from the U.S.A.?"

"Because," he replied, "I was told the American government did not allow Japanese to become citizens through naturalization."

Thus in 1910 Mr. Shimizu came to Vancouver. When he learned that the Grand Trunk Railway Company had begun building the Trans Canada Railway's northern route from Prince Rupert to Montreal, he headed for Prince Rupert to find a job. At that time the Canadian Pacific Railway had a thirty-year history and this new railway was to open the northern part of Canada, running about 200 or 300 miles north of the C.P.R. In 1914 the new railway was completed. Unfortunately the completion of the railway coincided with the outbreak of World War I and the resultant economic slump made it very difficult to maintain the new railway. And in 1918 the railway went bankrupt. However, the Canadian government purchased it and named it the Canadian National Railway which, of course, still exists.

"Can you tell me something about the prosperous restaurant business you had before the evacuation?" I asked.

"We established a restaurant with Mr. I. Nishikaze who was a good cook. He spent all his life as a cook. Together with this restaurant I had a hotel too. The name of the restaurant was the 'Dominion Cafe'. The total investment for our business was estimated at $80,000 at that time."

During the Second World War the Canadian government confiscated their entire establishment and gave them only $20,000 for it — one quarter of its real value. All the hard labour and hopes of 25 years vanished before their eyes.

The government forced all Japanese Canadians in the Prince Rupert area, numbering 606, to move to Vancouver's Hastings Park, herding them into the stalls where cattle were kept just a few months previous for the exhibition. The Shimizus were moved to an internment camp in New Denver, B.C. in 1942 and in 1946 they settled further east in Edmonton, Alberta. They did not go back to Prince Rupert because of the government's restrictions against Japanese returning to the coast.

"In order to leave the ghost town we all had to have jobs," said Mr. Shimizu, "so we worked at Misericordia Hospital in Edmonton at first. Then with the $20,000 we received for our property in Prince Rupert we started a business of housekeeping rooms and apartments — and finally we bought a house which proved to be quite valuable."

For many years Mr. Shimizu has suffered a great deal as a result of his blindness.

"When did you find out that your eyesight was going?" I asked.

"It was 1951 when I was 61 years old. I went to Lake Louise with our son Kenny and when I saw the lake it seemed very muddy due to my eye trouble. Within a year I became a totally blind man."

"You lived in Prince Rupert for so long. Is there anything you'd like to tell us about life there?"

"I was young and full of energy. For 25 years Mr.

Nishikaze and I worked together. This is indeed a remarkable thing. I married and a son was born, but unfortunately my young wife became very ill with Spanish flu and passed away in 1918. Then I married Kimiko. (Mrs. Kimiko Shimizu is a graduate of Heian Jogakuen, an Anglican girls school in Kyoto. She was a wonderful wife, a very kind person.) There were several Japanese families already there in Prince Rupert — the Yamanakas, Mochidas and Nishikazes — also the Suga, Hayakawa, and Kanaya families. A few years later the Matsumoto, Tsumura, and Suehiro families joined us.''

"I understand that you donated Japanese cherry trees to the city of Prince Rupert."

"I wanted to help beautify our city, so I ordered 3,000 cherry trees from Japan and donated them to the city. However, as you know, Prince Rupert is a very rocky place and due to the lack of deep soil the trees could not survive. It was unfortunate, but my spirit will remain there."

Mr. and Mrs. Shimizu loved the city of Prince Rupert. They loved the people, especially those of their own community. Through the enthusiastic efforts of the Shimizus and their friends, a beautiful Japanese cultural hall was built, providing a lively centre for Japanese Canadian activities. Most of the Japanese in Prince Rupert were members of St. Andrew's Japanese Anglican Mission. Mr. Shimizu remembers all the missionaries — Mr. Z. Higashi, Rev. A. Ban, Dr. Eleanor Lennox, (a missionary who came back from Japan) Rev. Tadashi Matsumoto, Miss K. Lang and Miss Withers.

"Have you any advice to give those who will follow in your footsteps?" I asked him.

"Yes." he said. "I think it's important to understand and love the people of the country where we live. As Canada is a country based on Christianity, it is easier and best to believe in Jesus Christ and to be a faithful member of the church. We always had a close relationship with the Bishop of the Diocese of Caledonia, and the Cathedral Church of St. Andrew's in Prince Rupert."

After they moved to Edmonton, Mr. and Mrs. Shimizu

expressed their love and appreciation for their new home by ordering 3,000 lilac trees from Sapporo, Japan and donating them to the city of Edmonton. Later Alberta and Hokkaido, Japan, became sister provinces. The lilacs of Sapporo actually originated in the United States, as the famous Dr. Clark of the University of Hokkaido, who influenced early Japanese Protestant Christianity, brought the trees from the U.S. and Sapporo was one of the few places where the lilacs would grow.

Shotaro Shimizu's dream of leaving his offspring in North America was realized. Today the Shimizu's second son, Dr. Henry Shimizu, is an outstanding plastic surgeon in Edmonton. He is not only past president of the Canadian Plastic Surgeon's Association, but also a recipient of the Queen Elizabeth Silver Jubilee medal. The Shimizu's younger son, Kenneth Kaien Shimizu, Ph.D., is a consultant architect in Vancouver, while their daughter lives in Toronto with her husband, Dr. Sakamoto. Their eldest son is in Toronto as well.

"You must have a lot of interesting stories to tell about the early days," I remarked as my visit with the Shimizu's was nearing its end.

"Yes, there are a lot of interesting stories but I will tell you just one," replied Mr. Shimizu. "One of my friends went to Japan to find a bride. He happened to meet a nice young woman who asked him many questions about himself. She asked him where he worked and he immediately replied, "In the office of a big, government railway." Believing that he held a high position in the railway, she accepted his proposal of marriage. But what a shock to discover when she came to Canada, that he was only a janitor in the big C.N.R. office. Somehow they both lived happily for many years. And now they have passed away . . ."

Genzo Kitagawa C.M.
First Japanese Canadian
Invested into The Order of Canada

In order to honour outstanding citizens, the Canadian govern-
ment established the "Order of Canada." Among the many reci-
pients are several Japanese Canadians, and the first was none
other than my close friend, Mr. Genzo Kitagawa of Regina, a
highly successful businessman, a leader of the Japanese com-
munity in Regina.

Unfortunately he passed away in 1976. His widow, Mrs.
Kikuno Kitagawa sent their memoirs and newspaper clippings
from which the following is taken.

Genzo Kitagawa came to Canada from Shiga-ken, Japan in
April 1911 at the age of fourteen, called here by his father.
He began working in a sawmill near Vancouver and attended
night school to learn English.

"Working conditions for us immigrants," he wrote
"were controlled by a Japanese 'straw-boss', who was the
interpreter, authority and general agent in charge. He
deducted his commission from our wages, which went
directly to him from the company. Our daily wages came to
seventy-five cents, lower than for the white workers. We had
enough white rice for our meals, but anything other than
that was inadequate and we were required to supplement our
meals at our own expense. Generally in those days new
Japanese immigrants were exploited.

"Some years later, I found work as a bell-boy in the
Hotel Vancouver, which gave me more money for less hard
labour. In 1917, I came to Calgary to work in the Hotel
Palliser as a bell-boy. When the Prince of Wales, later Duke
of Windsor, visited one of his ranches in Alberta, he stayed
at the Palliser Hotel. I was the bell-boy in charge of serving
him and it seems the Prince preferred that arrangement.

"In September 1922, I met Mr. Sataro Kuwabara of
Mission City, B.C., a former co-worker in Hotel Vancouver

who was now managing his own farm and attempting to build an independant business in this country.

"We had days and evenings of endless and searching discussions about what kind of business we might try and finally we thought of a joint project — a store in Calgary, handling imported goods from Japan. We had in mind the Christmas season of 1922.

"Uncertain and doubtful, but full of youth and ambition, we squeezed in time from our regular jobs and began our business venture. "The Nippon Bazaar" was opened on November 19, 1922 on 820 First Street West, Calgary, Alberta. We were in the midst of the depression of the twenties but when Christmas was over we had made a net profit of $800. It was a successful venture by the standards of the times.

" 'What next?' we wondered. Again we discussed plans. Our previous thought had been to close the store after Christmas, but we revised our plans and it was decided that I should work full time in the store, withdrawing from hotel work, while Mr. Kuwabara would conclude his farming venture in Mission City, B.C. and move to Calgary.

"In 1923, Mr. Shigejiro Inouye, a former Japanese Language School teacher in Vancouver, who was now working in the Palliser Hotel joined our partnership. Later we became a partnership of three stores — Kuwabara in Calgary, Kitagawa in Regina, Saskatchewan, and Inouye in Edmonton, Alberta. Although we have prospered, I remember when in the midst of the depression, a day's total sale was thirty-five cents in our store.

"Our main commodities for sale were small imported goods, toys, china, etc. Then gradually, beautiful silk yard-goods from Japan, which made a fine showing in our storefront exhibits, helped improve our business marvellously.

"In the depression years of 1922-23, when the Japanese yen was at its lowest rate of exchange, our business in Canada was ironically helped a great deal. Towards the end of 1924, our store was known and recognized as a good silk-goods store in Calgary. Also by this time we three were working in the store full time, Kuwabara as president drawing a salary of $100 a month and Inouye and myself as directors receiving $75 each. We kept our salaries at the lowest level as we were considering the expansion of our business in the future. (While working in the hotel, I had managed to save $100 a month and spent an equal amount for daily expenses.)

"Our living conditions in those days, aside from our business venture, was less than poor. The apartment where we stayed was like a poor-house. There was never hot water enough to bath. The hallway was always dark. Half of the lights were out of order. The windows in winter were ice. When looking back now, I wonder how Inouye with his family of four children was able to endure the conditions, even though it was for a short time.

"We worked long hours, from early in the morning to late at night seven days a week. By 1926, the business was established to our satisfaction. The time had come to plan our expansion beyond Calgary. We made trips east, to Swift Current, Regina, Saskatoon and Edmonton and reached a consensus on locating a new store at Regina.

"About this time, Mr. Tokujiro Wakabayashi while working at the Empire Hotel in Calgary came closer to our partnership.

"In 1926, I went to Japan, married Kikuno and returned to Calgary. Mabel was born in 1928 and in August, 1929, we moved to Regina. In September of 1929, we opened a branch store in Regina. I was in charge and Mr. Wakabayashi was my assistant. The name of the store was "Nippon Silk" and was located at 2419 11th Avenue. We had a five year lease with rent at $150 a month. We had heard that Eaton's was to build their large new store near by at the corner of 11th Avenue and Albert Street and it seemed an ideal spot for us.

"Our first five years in Regina were smooth and favourable, with not much in the way of profits, but no losses, and our long hours of work continued. During these years we expanded our space with Sommerset block where we were located.

"Mr. Wakabayashi left the company in 1934 and moved to Saskatoon to open his own business. In 1934 we moved to larger premises in Darke Block, 2125 — 11th Avenue, adding ladies fashion goods to our merchandise. That year, overseas, the China Incident began, the undeclared war between China and Japan, which led to the Manchurian War and to the Pacific War. It was an unpopular situation for us from the beginning. There were boycotts against Japanese goods and groups demonstrated from time to time at our store front. Irritation against us however did not much affect our daily business and gradually it faded away.

"One cold morning in November, 1935, on the way to the store, I found some of the city's red fire engines stationed near our store. While I was wondering where the fire was located, I found it to be at our store. Surprise and anxiety filled me. The cause of the fire has never been determined.

"The partnership gathered in Regina to face the problem, however fire sales and insurance coverage contributed to the repair and rebuilding of the facilities. And with a new store and new stocks, our business venture continued.

"In 1941, our fears became a reality. The war of the Pacific began in December. Our store's name was changed to "Silk-O-Lina" to avoid unnecessary public harrassment. Although our feelings were unstable, our business conditions improved. As the war in Europe and Asia progressed, commercial goods shortages became general. Most businesses flourished as long as supplies continued and our store was not an exception.

"In 1944, Darke Block was sold to Medical Arts, a company organized by a few doctors, and we had to find a new location. We overcame some struggles with the war time regulations and restrictions and settled in a building located on 1763 Scarth Street and business continued during the war years and beyond to the booming 60's."

Three more stores were opened, in 1964, 1967 and 1975. Earlier in 1973, Mr. Genzo Kitagawa, along with 54 other distinguished Canadians including Phil Esposito and Karen Magnussen, received the Order of Canada from Governor General Roland Michener. On May 22, 1976, after a two days illness, he died at the age of 73. Until those last two days, he had been making his daily rounds of the branch stores, as manager and director, faithfully fulfilling his role in his business partnership in his adopted country. At the time of his passing there were sixteen "Silk-O-Lina" stores in Regina, Saskatoon, Edmonton and Calgary.

Iwakichi Sugiyama
Industrialist

Among the few Japanese Canadian pioneers in industry we find such successful persons as Mr. Iwakichi Sugiyama and his partner, Mr. Senkichi Fukuyama. One day in the spring of 1982, I visited Iwakichi Sugiyama and his wife at their home on Willow Street in Vancouver where they live a peaceful and comfortable life of retirement. Here is a brief biography of Iwakichi Sugiyama, one strong-willed man who managed to start again, after the Second World War, from scratch and build up a successful fishing company which is still thriving today in the hands of his eldest son, James Shunichi.

Iwakichi Sugiyama was born on November 11, 1891 in Shimizu-shi, Shizuoka-ken, Japan. After finishing high school in 1905, he attended night school for four years in order to learn English. In 1912 he emigrated to Canada and soon went to work at Britannia Beach where there was a mine. Then three years later he left Britannia Beach to try his luck in the fishing industry with Mr. Senkichi Fukuyama as his partner. Using the money which Mr. Sugiyama had saved while working at Britannia Beach, the two men bought and installed an engine in a boat they built which they named "Hudson No. 1."

From 1915 until 1918 their business progressed favourably, so that by the end of 1918 Mr. Sugiyama had enough money to make a trip to Japan to get married. In 1919 he married Chiyo Kishiyama in Shimizu and the same year he returned to Canada with his bride.

Iwakichi Sugiyama soon became a prominent figure in the Japanese Canadian community in Vancouver. He was not only elected president of Shizuoka Kenjin kai (an association of immigrants of Shizuoka prefecture of Japan who were residing in Canada) for five years, but he also served as the president of a Japanese Language School in Vancouver from 1934 until 1941 when the school was forced to close. Also, in 1937 he was made a life member of the Red Cross of Japan.

Prior to the evacuation Sugiyama and Fukuyama had established three companies: Burrard Fish Co. Limited, Howe Sound Fisheries Limited and Canadian Saltery Limited. They also had a wholesale fish market on Campbell Avenue in Vancouver and were involved in the packing and exporting of salmon and herring.

After Japan bombed Pearl Harbour in 1941 the prosperous business of these two fishermen came to an abrupt end, as they were evacuated from the coast. Their three companies were sold or given away. Burrard Fish Company Limited and the wholesale fish market on Campbell Avenue were handed over to a man named Eddy Moir, along with all their equipment. Howe Sound Fisheries Limited and the salmon fishing and export enterprise at Alert Bay were given to S. Cook. The Canadian Saltery Ltd. plant at Galiano Island, B.C. on twenty acres of land was sold to Millard Company, along with all equipment on the premises, including two fifty-ton scows and five seine nets — all this for only $5,000. Today the value of this property and equipment would be worth millions of dollars. In addition to the above, Mr. Sugiyama and Mr. Fukuyama also had eight boats — Howe Sound 1 (1915), Howe Sound II (1918), Howe Sound III (1919), Howe Sound IV (1925), Howe Sound V (1940), Orca (1929), Menzies Bay (1927) and Sealuck (1929) — as well as two trucks. Except for four of the boats, the Canadian government took these valuable boats and trucks and sold them without the owner's consent at give away prices. What a sad thing the Canadian government did in the name of the War Measures Act.

Some time after the Japanese Canadians were permitted to return to the Pacific coast Mr. and Mrs. Sugiyama and their family came back to Vancouver to start their fishing industry once more. So it was that their enterprise sprang up again. Everything ran smoothly and in 1970 Mr. Sugiyama retired, handing over his company to his eldest son.

In November 1969, Mr. and Mrs. Sugiyama happily celebrated their fifty year golden wedding anniversary and in November 1979 their sixty year diamond wedding anniversary surrounded by their four sons and thirteen grandchildren.

During my visit with Mr. Sugiyama he showed me a document issued on May 14th, 1942 by the British Columbia Security Commission, Vancouver, B.C. It reads as follows:

Commission Permit No. 01054

Japanese Registration No. 05162, 05161, 07672, 13043.
This permit authorizes Mr. Iwakichi Sugiyama No. 05162, his wife No. 05161 and their four sons, Shunichi No. 07672, Shigeru and Shohei and Ryoji, 2704 Trinity Street, Vancouver, B.C., to travel in accordance with the provision of Orders-in-Council No. P.C. 1665 and 365 to farm property situated at Barnhurt Vale, B.C. (approx. 16 miles from Kamloops).
They must travel by rail, leaving Vancouver by May 25th, and must not re-enter the Restricted Area. This Commission assumes no responsibility for the cost of education of children of school age. They are to travel at their own expense and are to be self-supporting.

Signed C. G. MacNeil
for British Columbia Security Commission

Note: Shunichi Sugiyama is not travelling on this permit, but has permission to remain and complete his Matriculation Exams at Britannia High School, and travel later.

This Permit is not valid unless signed by one of the following authorized signatories:

Austin C. Taylor......................Chairman,
F. J. Mead............................Member,
John Shirras..........................Member,
Grant MacNeil ....Secretary.

This permit clearly demonstrates the fact that the education of the Sugiyama children had to be completed at their own expense. Even though their eldest son, James Shunichi, graduated from grade 13 in Vancouver, it was difficult for him to enroll in any university because most universities refused to accept Japanese Canadians — and even if a university itself accepted him, the city would refuse. Finally, the University of Manitoba at Winnipeg accepted Shunichi, yet he had to study at a college in Regina for a year. Lodging was another problem. But through the help of a professor's recommendation, he was able to find room and board at the home of a white Canadian family. In a short time he proved himself to be an intelligent and conscientious youth, so the family welcomed eight more Japanese students into their home. The father of the house was a painter and during the summer vacation he gave the students painting jobs which greatly eased their financial situations.

Despite all the anti-Japanese obstacles which they had to face in Canadian society, the four Sugiyama sons managed to excel at university and succeed in their chosen professions. Each was unable to enter UBC, even Dr. Henry Sugiyama who had won a scholarship to UBC but was refused admission. Today the eldest son, James Shunichi is the president of Sugiyama Company Limited in Vancouver; Jerry Shigeru is a mechanical engineer in Vancouver; the third son, Dr. Henry Shohei Sugiyama, is practising medicine in Toronto and the fourth son, George Ryoji, is a dentist in Vancouver.

Iwakichi Sugiyama was granted Canadian citizenship in 1921. But no Japanese Canadian was permitted to vote due to a clause in the Vancouver City charter which stated, "No

Japanese is entitled to vote''. However, Mr. Sugiyama soon discovered an obvious loophole in this anti-Japanese charter. One paragraph stated that "No Chinaman, Hindu, Japanese or Indian shall be entitled to vote at any municipal election", but the next paragraph stated that "in case of a corporation voting through its authorized agent, such agent shall be entitled to vote — until his authorization shall have been cancelled by his company." A further clause stipulated that the agent "must be a resident of British Columbia and a British subject."

Armed with this evidence, Mr. Iwakichi Sugiyama, manager of Burrard Fish Co. Ltd., appeared before Revising Judge J. M. Richardson and presented his credentials as the official representative of his company — and as a British subject. The court had no option but to order that the company's name be placed on the voters' list. Thus the Vancouver newspaper reported that Mr. Iwakichi Sugiyama was the only Japanese who voted at the civic election in 1940.

"Have you any advice to give the following generation?" I asked Mr. and Mrs. Sugiyama.

"I want our following generations to be honest, industrious and trustworthy, as we were to our neighbours and friends in Canada, and to prosper in their lives," replied Mr. Sugiyama smiling.

Fred Masuyei Tamagi

Masuyei Fred Tamagi
Founder of Bridge Brand Food Services

"From a used Ford truck and a market garden, to a Cadillac-class Total Supply Distribution Centre in twenty-five years . . ." This is a quotation from a special issue of the *Calgary Albertan*, October 1973, celebrating the 25th anniversary of Bridge Brand Food Services, now the largest independent food service business in Canada.

My relationship with the pioneer founder, F. M. Tamagi goes back to the time of the government's dispersal policy when interned Japanese Canadians were spread across Canada. It was August 30, 1945 when my family and I arrived in Coaldale, Alberta following our three years in the internment camp of Slocan City, B.C. I had been sent to Southern Alberta by the Missionary Society of the Church of England in Canada (M.S.C.C.) to begin an Anglican Japanese Mission among the approximately 4,200 people who were relocated there as sugar beet labourers.

There were a number of factors that influenced our going to Coaldale. 1. The nearby city of Lethbridge where I first desired to go refused us entry due to anti-Japanese sentiments. 2. The village of Coaldale consisting of a majority population of Mennonites welcomed us. 3. A newly converted Christian from Coaldale named Masuyei Fred Tamagi persuaded me to come to Coaldale to begin a mission. We met and became life long friends.

One of the Tamagi boys, William, popularly known as Billy was a much beloved and gifted member of the Coaldale community, known to many people as an entertaining public speaker, counsellor, singer and writer. He was ordained to the United Church ministry and served in Southern Alberta and Honolulu, Hawaii. He is now vice president of Bridge Brand and has offered the following sketch of his parents.

In 1908 (or thereabouts), an ambitious young Japanese left the island of Okinawa and headed west to make his mark, stopping first in Hawaii where he amassed the small

Kanako Tamagi

fortune of $3,000 and set out for Canada, the Land of Opportunity. Apparently, while in Hawaii, he learned the art of running a movie-projector and planned to return to Okinawa to enter into the movie house business, but was encouraged by his father to go on to Canada.

Masuyei Fred Tamagi was born in 1891 at Higa Island, Okinawa, Japan. He arrived in Vancouver, B.C. in 1912, bought a pool hall and leaving his older brother in charge, went back to Japan to pick a bride, Kanako Uehara. They returned to Vancouver only to find that the business had gone broke: and it was there where their first daughter, Yeiko Marline was born. The Tamagis then proceeded on to Calgary, Alberta, where he found work with the Canadian Pacific Railroad and also enrolled in a barber school to learn the trade.

Another daughter, Fumiko Winnifred was born in Edson, Alberta, around that time. The Tamagis then moved to Raymond, Alberta, where he set up his first Barber Shop. Subsequently, a restaurant business was purchased which was given the name, the Togo Cafe. It was here in Raymond, the heart of the Mormon community and the location of the first Mormon Temple in Canada, that four sons were born, Kazuo Kenneth, Yoshiharu William, Yeichi James, and Masayuki Samuel. Around this time, the parents felt it advisable to send the three oldest (Yeiko, Fumiko and Kazuo) back to Okinawa, to be cared for by the grandparents until they became financially established, and able to support their growing family.

The next move took them to Diamond City, where Mrs. Tamagi ran a boarding house, and father Tamagi worked in the coal mine and set up a confectionary and ice cream parlor, again showing his preference and talent for being involved in private business ventures. Two more boys were born, Keigo (who passed away in infancy) and Fred (Igo), their youngest son.

Hardieville, a little village about 6 miles from the city of Lethbridge became the next stop. Mr. Tamagi took a job in the No. 6 coal mine there, and called his two oldest daughters aged thirteen and eleven from Japan. He taught them the barbering trade, and they commuted between Hardieville and Lethbridge while running the new barbershop in the city. With the advent of the 1930's near at hand, the family moved to Lethbridge to be close to the thriving barbershop business.

In 1928, the price of potatoes skyrocketed to $50 per ton, and father Tamagi quickly bought an eighty-acre farm in Coaldale twelve miles east of Lethbridge, and harvested a bumper crop to cash in on the prairie "gold strike" (so to speak). But he had not considered Black Friday and the Wall Street stock market crash in October of 1929. The price of potatoes dropped to $5 per ton, and they were thrown into the depression of the "Dirty Thirties".

Then followed a decade of struggle which found the Tamagi family barely ekeing out their physical existence, often subsisting on young dandelion greens and a couple of tins of sardines, bought for two cents per tin, which mother Tamagi made into a palatable salad. The only meat they ate were pigeons which their young sons knocked down from the rafters in the barn with slingshots. However, undaunted, Mr. Tamagi managed to buy an old 1936 Ford truck and began peddling potatoes and garden produce from town to town throughout Southern Alberta with his sons, while Mrs. Tamagi took care of the harvesting of the vegetables at home. It was her ingenuity and management of their meagre savings that resulted in the purchase of a small acreage on the outskirts of the town of Coaldale, and that finally resulted in the building of the first warehouse in Calgary in 1948. This small building covered 500 sq. ft. of space on two floors. (Equipment and staff consisted of one truck and 3 employees). It is an interesting fact that the lot for this first building was purchased with a loan of $600 from Rev. Gordon G. Nakayama, who became lifelong friends of the Tamagis.

As a matter of interest, while in Coaldale, during the difficult days immediately following Pearl Harbour and the subsequent evacuation of the Japanese from the west coast to relocation camps in the interior of B.C. and the farms of southern Alberta, Mr. Tamagi rendered a valuable service to the authorities and assisted in the orderly relocation of the displaced families by acting as interpreter for the R.C.M.P.

The establishing of the warehouse in Calgary was preceded by a little business venture involving a fruit and vegetable stall in the City Hall Market, manned by their two oldest girls, Yeiko and Fumiko and son, James Yeichi. This successful operation provided the basis and impetus for the beginning of a most successful distribution operation which eventually became Canada's largest independent foodservice business. The youngest daughter, Shirley was born in Calgary in 1936, where the whole family eventually moved.

Bridge Brand Food Services now occupies a master distribution center at 1802 Centre Avenue N.E. in Calgary, boasting over 180,000 sq. ft. of prime warehouse facilities, with 26 loading docks. Specializing in total supply for the entire food service industry, Bridge Brand handles over 5,000 products and services over 2,000 accounts, hospitals, hotels, nursing homes, restaurants, etc. There is also a branch in the city of Red Deer, 90 miles to the north of Calgary.

The parents are both deceased now, Mr. Tamagi in 1960 and Mrs. Tamagi in 1975. The story of Mr. and Mrs. Fred Tamagi would not be complete without telling of the incident that sparked his conversion to Christianity. It was the time of the Second World War and Mr. Tamagi had bought a number of cases of liquor, keeping them in the basement of their house in Coaldale. He was hoping to invite RCMP officers and others for a New Year's party. Their son, Bill who was then a Salvation Army Officer, found the liquor and out of concern for his mother's welfare, he risked his father's rage and threw the entire contents into the out-house. Mr. Tamagi was furious, but Bill with tears in his eyes begged him to stop drinking. His son's courage was the beginning of Father Tamagi's conversion.

F. M. Tamagi and Sons has become a huge business enterprise and future generations will no doubt marvel at the rapid success that was effected in one lifetime.

Masajiro Miyazaki, Nov. 1976

Masajiro Miyazaki C.M.
Physician

Among a few Japanese Canadians who are members of the Order of Canada, we find Dr. Masajiro Miyazaki of Lillooet, B.C. His book, 'My Sixty Years in Canada', is in its fourth printing and is available from the Kamloops J. C. Citizen's Association, 1724 Clifford Avenue, Kamloops, B.C., V2B 4G6.

I was born on November 24, 1899 (Meiji 32) in a farming village of Kaideima, near Hikone City, Shiga-ken, Japan. I came to Vancouver on the S.S. Empress of India with my father who was returning to Canada after a short visit home. It was June 29, 1913 and I was taken to our friend's house on 500 block Powell Street. As soon as I was settled, my father left for Skeena to go fishing. At that time Powell Street from Main Street to Princess Avenue was filled with Japanese stores, rooming houses, bath houses, a bank, two Chinese chop suey houses and a movie theatre. There were half a dozen saw mills on the shores of False Creek and many Japanese workers lived in the Fairview section. To get there from Powell Street, one had to cross False Creek over the Main Street wooden bridge. What is now the C.N. station and Industrial Park was a mud flat and it was filled with sand dredged from False Creek in 1920. I remember burning boxes to make a big bonfire on the sandy flat when I was initiated as freshman at U.B.C. in 1921.

When I arrived in Canada I was unable to speak a word of English. So during July and August I attended the English class of Sister Maria, known to Japanese as Omeria-san. When school opened in September, my English was good enough for my admission to grade three, or the first Reader class of Strathcona School. At that time there were only six Japanese pupils attending Strathcona, whereas by the time of the evacuation there were six hundred Japanese children at Strathcona. In 1913 most Japanese children attended regular Japanese school, the Kokumin Gakko on Alexander Street and learned English after Japanese school was over. While going to Strathcona, I found an 'after school' job at Taishodo Drug store which paid my board and gave me some spending money. From this time on I was on my own.

After staying in Vancouver for a year I transferred to New Westminster and worked as a school boy domestic in a private home and attended John Robson Public School and Duke of Connaught High School. During the summer vacation I took leave of absence and worked as a saw mill hand.

When I finished my first year in high school in 1921, I was called to Vancouver by the Canadian Japanese Association to receive the $25 scholarship for university students. (The High School scholarship was $15.) Considering that U.B.C. tuition was $40 a year, the scholarship was a great help.

In September 1919, the Japanese Students Club was formed and after the organization meeting was held in Kokumin Gakko, we posed for a picture which is now preserved in Dr. Miyazaki's Special Collection at the U.B.C. library. The first president was Mr. Kosaburo Shimizu, of Arts '19. I became president in 1923 and served till my graduation in 1925. While attending U.B.C. I supported myself by working as caretaker at the Third Avenue Japanese Anglican Mission and by teaching English to new immigrants from Japan. When I graduated in 1925, I was the seventh Japanese to graduate from U.B.C. but the only Japanese to graduate from a university in Canada that year. I graduated from the old 'Fairview shack' which was our university before it was moved to Point Grey in September, 1925. Earlier, in 1922, I had taken part in the 'Great Trek', the campaign to have the university moved to Point Grey.

My ambition was to become a physician but when I tried to enter medical school, many obstacles lay in my path because of my race. One of the schools would not accept me because non-whites couldn't serve as interns in the hospitals. One medical school in Michigan was willing to accept me but the American Immigration Board wanted me to put up a large cash bond which I didn't have. Finally a school in Missouri offered to put up the bond so I went to Kirksville College of Osteopathic Medicine, Missouri, U.S.A. While there, I worked as a bus boy in the hotel dining room and during Christmas and summer holidays, I worked as waiter at a country club in St. Louis. Thus I was able to support myself and had to borrow only a small amount.

I graduated in May 1929 and returned to Vancouver to take the Medical Board examination for a licence to practice in B.C. Though I received the licence in September 1929, I did not open the office right away. Instead, I went to Los Angeles for further training and worked at the Mexican Hospital in L.A. I opened my office for private practice in May 1930 and practiced until August 1942 when I was evacuated to Bridge River, B.C.

Today, it is easy for Nisei and Sansei to find jobs in their chosen fields but it wasn't so in the twenties when we Issei graduated from U.B.C. Many left for Japan to work there. Junichi Hokkyo, Arts '20, Seiji Tamenaga, Science '21, Haruo Yonemoto, Arts '23, Susumu Kobe, Arts '26, Noboru Nakano, Arts '26, Fred Maikawa, Arts '28 and Rigenda Sumida all went to Japan as they couldn't get jobs in Canada. Chitose Uchida Arts '16 had to go to Alberta to teach as the school boards in B.C. would not hire her. The only Japanese who was hired was Hide Hyodo, Arts '28, who was hired by the Richmond school board as there were so many Japanese pupils in grade one who couldn't speak English. These days many Niseis and Sanseis are teachers and principals. In 1970 when NorKam Secondary School was seeking a vice principal, there were 30 applicants, including my daughter Betty Inouye. The choice was narrowed to six candidates and finally my daughter was chosen. Imagine a Japanese Canadian girl beating 29 other white male candidates. This could not have happened in the 30's when racial discrimination was still rampant.

When Shinobu Higashi and Tommy Shoyama graduated in 1938, they had difficulty finding jobs. When I was in Ottawa to receive the Order of Canada medal, I was invited to brunch by Kunio Shimizu and Tommy Shoyama who was at that time the Deputy Minister of Finance and when I mentioned that my son Kenneth who graduated with his B.Com. in 1977 from U.B.C., was working for the Price Waterhouse accounting firm, Tommy Shoyama told me that when he graduated and looked for work, he went to Price Waterhouse as well as other firms but no one would hire him. Forty years later, my son had offers from three firms.

But back in 1938, Tommy Shoyama's fellow graduate, Shinobu Higashi was planning to go north to work as a bull cook in a lumber camp. He couldn't find a job so I decided to create one for him. I was talking to Mr. Maeba of Taiyo Printing Co. who was complaining about the scarcity of business in the printing field. So it gave me an idea. Why not start an English language paper for the Niseis and let Taiyo Printing Co. print it. That would also bring in steady business for Taiyo. I called a few of my friends to my office and discussed the possibility of starting an English language paper for Japanese Canadians. Everybody agreed with the idea. Since Taiyo printing was willing to provide a corner of their printing shop and the use of a telephone there wasn't much expense to start. Shinobu Higashi was to be editor, reporter, subscription and ad salesman. Ed Ouchi, who was in the insurance business was to look after finances. I gave $10 and Dr. Saita $5 to start publishing *The New Canadian*, which is still in business and is read by Japanese Canadians across Canada. Very few people know how the paper was started. Higashi's ability was recognized by the *Manchurian Daily* and shortly afterwards Shinobu left for Mukden to work for the *Manchurian Daily*. His brother Yoshimitsu took his place and later still Tommy Shoyama became editor and was in charge of the paper at the time of the evacuation. As Japanese language papers had been banned, the B.C. Security Commission had difficulty in communicating with the Isseis so *The New Canadian* became a bilingual paper as it is today.

When we formed the Japanese Students' Club in 1919 it was made up of High School and University students, but soon the numbers increased and U.B.C. formed its own Japanese Students' Club. Their monthly meetings were often held at my house and my wife and I used to attend their dances as chaperones. In 1937 I organized the Japanese Alumni Association of U.B.C. and became its first president serving till 1941.

In 1934 I was elected to the Council of the Canadian Japanese Association and served until the evacuation of 1942. I became treasurer in 1938 and under my direction, membership increased from 4,000 to 5,000 members. I served as treasurer until 1941.

In 1940 I was called to Hotel Vancouver by the Hugh Keenleyside Commission as the representative of the Canadian Japanese Association because of my facility in English, though I was only a treasurer and the youngest member. Others present were delegates from the Japanese Chamber of Commerce, Fishermen's Union and Farmers' Union. Soon after this interview, the Canadian government commenced registration of all Japanese and thus knew the whereabouts of every Japanese in Canada. When war was declared in December 1941, the R.C.M.P. picked up forty Japanese. When the government started sending Japanese of military age to road camps in the Rockies, I was included among them, but when I presented myself at the R.C.M.P. barracks, I was told that because Japanese doctors were needed to look after the Japanese left behind, I didn't have to go to camp. I stayed behind and practiced until August. Towards the end of July, I was called to the office of Dr. Hodgens, the medical supervisor of the B.C. Security Commission. He suggested that I go to Bridge River to look after the Japanese evacuees there. I had no other choice. Had I refused, I would have been sent to a prisoner of war camp at Petawawa, Ontario.

On August 2nd, 1942, I packed my family in my car and drove to Bridge River. My household goods were sent by freight via P.G.E. Railway. My living quarters and office had been provided by the community and I started practicing among the Japanese evacuees. I had a three bed hospital to take care of maternity cases and was able to handle all those who came from Lillooet and Minto.

When the Indians in a nearby reserve found out there was a doctor available at Bridge River they wanted to come to me instead of travelling to Lillooet to see their Indian doctor. So the Indian Affairs Department started paying me for the visits of Indian patients. I delivered Indian babies at their reserves. I also delivered two babies of white women in Bridge River. When Dr. Paterson of Lillooet passed away some Lillooet people came to Bridge River for consultation. When the town of Lillooet couldn't get any doctor to come and set up practice, the B.C. Police came to see me and ask me if I wished to relocate. I was willing but the B.C. Security Commission wouldn't let me go unless I was welcomed by the townspeople, as the town of Lillooet was a "no Japanese allowed" town. A petition was then sent to the B.C. Security Commission and with the approval of the Commission and the Bridge River community our family moved to Lillooet on March 31, 1945. It was Mr. A. W. A. Phair, the secretary of the Lillooet Board of Trade who drafted the petition and who provided me with living quarters and an office in his large house. I bought the house in April 1947 when the ban was lifted.

I started treating the Indians of the Lillooet district on a per call basis but after three months the Indian agent wanted me to work on a monthly salary basis. Because I was doing more work than the former doctor, the Indian Affairs Department was willing to pay me more than double of what the former doctor was getting. As there was no hospital in Lillooet, I delivered all Indian babies in their homes in the reserve. The white people went to Lytton hospital for maternity cases, but sometimes they couldn't make it. In such cases I'd be called and I would deliver the babies in their homes. I encountered some very difficult cases and was without the aid of specialists in some very difficult circumstances. Some of the homes were only accessible by horseback along trails, or by rowboat or cable car ferry across the Fraser river. In the early days of my practice there was no road connection to Shalath or D'Arcy so I made use of the P.G.E. trains. When the trains were available I rode the train

or freight car. Sometimes I had to travel on the patrol
speeder or section speeder. Once I had a chance to travel on
the Executive's car when I met one of my classmates, who
was then superintendent of P.G.E. Another time I went to
Bridge River on a speed boat to attend a maternity case and
on another occasion I went to D'Arcy on a sea plane and was
able to get there in 20 minutes instead of two hours by
speeder. My big black bag was always filled with necessary
tools for any emergency operation and I did curettage operations on beds and other operations on kitchen tables.

Besides the general work of a country practitioner, I
also did work for the coroner and the police. Whenever a
patient died from an accident or without medical attention,
the coroner was called and I was asked to report on the cause
of death. In cases of murder or manslaughter I'd be called to
testify as medical witness at the trial. As a police doctor I
attended the prisoners in jail and examined and signed cer-
tificates before the prisoners were transferred to Oakalla.
Thus I had a very interesting country practice. No other
Japanese Canadian doctor ever had the opportunity I had as
police and coroner's doctor.

When the Pacific War ended in 1945, the Japanese in
the U.S. were allowed to return to the west coast, but the
Canadian government did not lift its restrictions. On April 1,
1947, the ban on purchase of property by the Japanese was
lifted and I was able to purchase our present house which
was built in 1878 and is the oldest house still standing in
Lillooet. Although the Chinese and Indians were granted
franchise in 1947, we Japanese had to wait two more years.
Finally on March 7, 1949 a bill was passed to repeal Section
12 of the Village Municipality Act. With the passing of this
bill which was assented to on March 24th the stigma of dis-
franchisement was at an end and with it a whole list of political and economic discrimination was washed away. From this
time on, we Japanese Canadians were able to vote and hold
public office.

Shortly after this act was passed, Lillooet was voting on
a referendum to build a new high school. As I was a property

owner and a Canadian citizen, I was entitled to vote on the money by-law. So I went to cast my ballot but the returning officer challenged me. He told me that I could not vote because I was a Japanese Canadian. In 1900 Tommy Honma tried to have his name put on the voters' list and when he was refused, he sued the registrar, won in the lower court but lost finally in Privy Council. Unlike Honma, I didn't have to sue the returning officer but told him that he was ignorant of the passage of the Amendment Act to the Village Municipality Act and told him to get in touch with Victoria and find out for himself. Of course the answer from Victoria was that I could vote, so I was given the ballot. I think I was the first Japanese Canadian to vote after the Amendment Act was passed. Next year the opportunity came for me to run for village commissioner (present alderman). So I became a candidate in the 1950 election. When I announced my candidacy it was news and when I was elected to the Council, the Canadian Press broadcast the news that I was the first Japanese Canadian to hold public office in all of Canada. I ran two more times and served for five years.

In 1951, the Lillooet Board of Trade entertained the Board of Trade delegates from Vancouver and sitting beside me at the table was an alderman from Vancouver. When I told him I was only a commissioner in a little village, he told me that my vote would count just as much as his at the municipal convention. As chairman of the health committee, I represented Lillooet at the Union Board of Health at Kamloops and my vote counted just as much as the alderman of Kamloops City which was thirty times as large as Lillooet.

When my church, St. Andrews United Church of Lillooet sponsored the Cubs and Scouts in 1959, I joined the scout movement and became treasurer of First Lillooet Group Committee of the Boy Scouts of Canada.

When Kumsheen District was organized in December 1964, I became its secretary-treasurer and badge secretary. I organized the training course for the leaders in our district and managed the District Cub and Scout camps. For my service to scouting, I was awarded the Medal of Merit from the Governor General, Roland Mitchener, Chief Scout of Canada. The investiture ceremony took place in Vancouver and the medal was presented by Lieutenant Governor John Nicholson. The citation read as follows: "In his triple capacity as Secretary-Treasurer and Badge Secretary of the Kumsheen District Council — a District stretching over 200 miles in length — he has contributed personal time, effort and resources in giving direction to the members of the District. Through his initiative and untiring dedication, his is the strongest rural District in the Interior Region. His residence is always 'open house' to scouters, whether enroute through his community or attending local training courses, as well as to hosting many scout groups. He has been instrumental in acquiring very desirable property for the scout movement. Dr. Miyazaki has performed his important functions for over nine years with effectiveness and efficiency and is highly respected for his devotion to Scouting."

In 1970 I had to go to Kamloops for treatment of my kidney ailment and I was there till 1972. While there I served as treasurer of Kamloops District council of Boy Scouts of Canada. When I returned to Lillooet in 1972, I became treasurer of the 1st Lillooet Group Committee again but after serving twenty years as treasurer, I resigned from the office of treasurer but kept my seat as Director of Interior Regional Council.

Besides my general practice, I found time to take part in many other activities. I was director of the Board of Trade and as chairman of the Health committee I promoted the ambulance service, organized the society in 1951 and became its first president. I conducted fund raising campaigns, bought the ambulance and directed the operation of ambulance services for nineteen years. The B.C. government operates the ambulance now but when we started, we were the only small village in B.C. which had an ambulance.

When Lillooet Lodge No. 467 of the Benevolent and Protective Order of Elks was instituted in 1961, I was a charter member and held many offices as Trustee,

Treasurer, Chaplain and Historian and the chairmanship of many committees.

In September 1970, the village of Lillooet and Elks Lodge put on a testimonial dinner for me and I came from Kamloops for the event. Elks Lodge made me an honourable life member and the village of Lillooet made me a Freeman of Lillooet which is the most honoured title any citizen could receive. There are about 600 Freeemen in Canada but I believe I am the only Japanese Canadian to receive this honour.

In 1973 I was elected president of Lillooet District Historical Society, which operates the Museum and the following year I became treasurer and served for six more years. When I resigned from the office of treasurer, I was made an Honourable Member in February 1979.

I joined the Lillooet Volunteer Fire Brigade when we had only a hose cart but while I was on the village council, I worked and obtained a fire truck and built a fire hall to house it.

The Order of Canada was established on July 1, 1967 the centennial year of the confederation of Canada. Acceptance into the Order is a great honour so I was quite surprised when I was notified that I had been admitted. On the morning of December 18, 1976, I received a phone call from Mr. Howard Johnstone M.P. of Ottawa, congratulating me and assuring me that he had seen my name among the list published by the Toronto *Globe and Mail.* When I went to the post office to get my mail, there was a registered letter from the Chancellery. Soon the U.B.C. Chronicle, Vancouver and Kamloops papers started phoning me for more information and my photos, and as the articles appeared in the papers, I was deluged with congratulatory messages, including one from Joe Clark, one from the B.C. Government, the regional, provincial and national councils of Boy Scouts of Canada and many others.

In April 1977 I was invited to the investiture ceremony in Ottawa. My daughter Betty Inouye and I flew from Kamloops on April 19th and checked in at the Skyline Hotel. A message was waiting for me from Mr. Johnstone who advised me of the activities arranged for the following days. The next day we met Mrs. Dale Johnstone in the lobby of the Parliament building. She guided us through the building and at noon we were guests of Mr. Johnstone at the M.P.'s restaurant. In the afternoon, we attended the session of parliament and observed from the gallery the workings of the M.P.'s during the Question Period.

In the evening, two buses transported the recipients and guests to Rideau Hall where the investiture ceremony was to take place. We were escorted to assigned seats in the Ball Room and when we were all seated with fanfare, their Excellencies entered the ballroom in procession. After the invocation, the names of recipients were called, and each one stepped forward and stood in front of Governor General Jules Leger while the citation was read. Then His Excellency placed the medal of the Order of Canada around the recipient's neck. The badge of the order is a cross with six enamelled white arms representing a snowflake, in the centre a maple leaf surrounded by a red enamelled ring, surmounted by the Royal Crown, and inscribed with the motto of the Order, DESIDERANTES MELIOREM PATRIAM (They Desire a Better Country). On the reverse of the badge is inscribed the word CANADA and a registration number. The ribbon of the Order is white with a broad red edge, representing the Canadian flag.

It is significant that exactly 100 years after the first Japanese immigrant Manzo Nagano stepped off the boat at Victoria in April 1877, another Japanese immigrant stood before the Governor General in Rideau Hall, in April 1977, to be honoured by Canada as a Canadian citizen, for his contribution to his adopted country.

Rintaro Hayashi, Leader
Among Japanese Canadian Fishermen

One day in April 1982, Mr. Kiyozo Kazuta of Vancouver and I took the Richmond bus and visited Mr. and Mrs. Rintaro Hayashi in their home in Steveston, B.C.

Mr. Rintaro Hayashi, an outstanding Japanese Canadian leader, contributed much to the welfare of Japanese Canadian fishermen. He was born in 1901 at Mio-mura, Wakayama-ken, Japan, the youngest of five children. He came to Canada at age twelve in 1913, called here by his father who was a fisherman in Steveston. He told me that there were about 2,000 Japanese in Steveston then. As soon as he came to Canada, he entered the Steveston Japanese School and attended the local public school as well.

Later Rintaro Hayashi, one of the founders of kendo in Canada, served as secretary of the Steveston Japanese Fishermen's Association. Included in the work of the Fishermen's Association was its financing of the Steveston Japanese Hospital. While he was secretary of the Association, he encountered many difficult problems related to the anti-Japanese movement in B.C. It was in 1911 that the Attorney General of B.C. published and publicized his contention that in order to protect the B.C. coastal area from a Japanese invasion, fishermen from England should replace Japanese fishermen who might serve as enemy agents. However, during the First World War the Japanese navy protected the B.C. coast, Japan being allies of Britain. When the war ended and post war depression became severe the ugly anti-Japanese movement started again. This time the politicians joined forces with the white fishermen, moving the government to regulate and reduce the issuing of fishing licences to Japanese Canadian fishermen from ten percent in 1920 to fifteen percent and finally forty percent in 1924. Japanese Canadian fishermen also lost the privilege of fishing in the off-limit international sea — that is, three miles off shore of the west coast of Vancouver Island, which had open fishing rights at that time. The Japanese Fishermen's Association fought the persecution, bringing the case to the Supreme Court of Canada and eventually to the Privy council of England. They won the case on October 15, 1929.

Mr. Hayashi worked faithfully as secretary until the outbreak of the Pacific War. The first Japanese Canadian victims of the persecution that followed in Canada were the fishermen. Their boats were confiscated by the Canadian Navy and they were ordered to head for the nearest port. The boats were then lashed together and dragged to the mouth of the Fraser River — a cruel act. The Canadian Navy treated Japanese Canadian fishermen as enemy seamen. It is hard to describe the hardships these men suffered. The men from the Skeena and the Nass River areas sailed their boats into Prince Rupert as they were ordered and when they arrived at Prince Rupert they were told that their destination was Vancouver. Without time to take fuel, food, or water, their boats were lashed together and dragged to Vancouver. For many days and nights they suffered from a lack of food and water. More than 1,200 Japanese fishing boats were assembled on the shores of Annacis Island and later these boats were sold without the consent of the owners at ridiculously low prices.

There were many things Mr. Hayashi could tell us about the pre-war days but not wanting to tire him as he had suffered a stroke about two years ago, I asked him, "What happened to your family at the time of the evacuation?"

"We were forced to leave our home," he said. "First we went to Kaslo, a ghost town in the interior of B.C., then we were sent to Lemon Creek, near Slocan City. Later we went to Raymond, Alberta where we worked on a sugar beet farm for two years. We moved to Kelowna, B.C. and finally back to Steveston in 1951 — two years after the restriction of returning to the B.C. coast was lifted."

"Would you tell me about some of your friends?" I asked.

"Yes, I've had many friends but as I find it hard to speak due to my stroke, you may read about them in my

159

book, *The Shores of the Black Current (Kuroshiro no Hate)*. In
it I have mentioned some of my friends," he answered.

In this book Mr. Hayashi mentions some important
Japanese Canadian pioneers such as: Mr. Ryuichi Yoshida,
who was the President of the Steveston Japanese Fishermen's Association and who contributed a great deal to the
welfare of Japanese in those days; Mr. Takejiro Oode, who
pioneered the salted herring industry and had a storage camp
at Nanaimo and Galiano Islands; Mr. Shintaro Takashima,
the first principal and teacher of the Steveston Japanese
School who taught many Japanese children including Mr.
Hayashi; Mr. James Tenning of Mie-ken Japan, whose real
name was Jujiro Takenouchi, a former Japanese Naval
officer, who came to Canada and was employed as secretary
of the Japanese Fishermen's Association; Mrs. Motoe
Yamazaki, who was the wife of Yasushi Yamazaki, the publisher and editor of the *Tairiku Nippo* newspaper. There were
many others referred to in the book but we are unable to
hear their stories as many of them have passed away.

My final question to him was, "Have you anything you
would like to tell our young people?"

"Oh yes," he replied. "There are some good and
important qualities of the old Japanese generation, the Issei
of the Meiji era, but there are also many undesirable things
too. We would like to leave behind us the good qualities,
such as honesty, sincerity, industriousness and trustworthi-
ness."

And I agreed that these good attributes should be kept.

Rintaro Hayashi married Yoshiko Nakano of Mio-
mura, Wakayama-ken, Japan in 1935. They have four
children and five grandchildren. Although he is not in good
health, Rintaro and his wife Yoshiko are enjoying a happy
retired life.

Shiro Koga
A Multi-talented Farmer and Engineer

From 1922 to 1923, I was a student of McLean High School in Maple Ridge and lived at the farm of Mr. and Mrs. Jiro Inouye, in the village of Port Haney, B.C. There were many Japanese strawberry farms in this area and Jiro Inouye, Yasutaro Yamaga, Shiro Oka, Yazaemon Tamura, and Shiro Koga were some of the pioneer strawberry growers. Mr. Shiro Koga was one of the leaders in the farming community and he was also a very talented, gifted man. The following is taken from a story written by his nephew, Mr. Uemon Koga, the manager of Japanese Social Services and Information Inc., of Los Angeles, California, U.S.A.

Shiro Koga was born February 7, 1885 in Saga-ken Japan. Although he had only a basic public school education he had many talents. He was a farmer, singer, actor, orator, engineer, and mechanical technician — all these accomplishments combined to make his life rich and colourful.

From early childhood he was devoted and faithful to his parents, particularly to his sick mother who suffered from arthritis. As a young boy he carried his mother on his back to the hot spring bath for treatment. It is said that such a faithful child would live a long life and so it was that he lived to be 89 years old.

He grew up during the time of the great Depression, just after the Russo-Japanese War. The whole nation suffered under severe economic depression. He had the heavy burden of helping to support his family and also to educate his brothers. Two of his brothers went on to medical school and became prominent physicians with their own private hospital, the other brother entered a theological college to become a Buddhist priest. After graduating from the theological college he went to study at the University of California in the United States of America.

The youth, Shiro Koga, never wasted his time. He devoted himself to hard and endless farm labour. Because of

161

the limited income from the farm, he had to find part-time work to increase his income. He raised silk worms, harvested and planted trees around the farm, etc. At night, after the heavy day's work had ended, he would get a group of people together to perform in theatrical plays or musical and dance concerts. It was customary for young people of his village to entertain at the village ceremonial services honouring the village shrine at various seasons of the year. Shiro was made responsible for the setting up of a huge fireworks display and on rainy days or at night when outdoor farm work could not be carried out, he devoted much of his time in the making and setting up of elaborate and ingenious fireworks displays. A few times a year, with the help of many talented youngsters, he set off the gigantic, spectacular fireworks which attracted a huge gathering of people. The success of his fireworks made him famous and many business contractors came offering him money.

In spite of his success in many fields of endeavour he was unable to meet all the family expenses, so he was at last compelled to go abroad. He chose Canada because his elder brother had already emigrated there and he thought that he and his brother together would be able to raise enough money to solve the financial difficulties at home. However, due to strict immigration laws he needed a sponsor in order to emigrate to Canada. Mr. Jiro Inouye, his brother's friend in Port Haney, B.C., offered to sponsor him and thus he was contracted to work for three years on the Inouye farm.

Shiro arrived in Canada in 1915 and after serving three long years of hard, farm work, he became a legal immigrant. He soon joined his brother who was a foreman of a resort at Bowen Island, B.C., and under his brother were many Japanese workers. This summer resort was a huge self-contained complex with large tracts of land along the bay and sea shore. There were tenting grounds, bungalows, a hotel, recreational areas, picnic and camping grounds, farm land for raising cattle and farm produce, a dance hall, grocery stores, etc.

The resort provided Shiro an ideal place to display and demonstrate his many skills and talent. Under his supervision a concrete dam was constructed and by using the lake as a reservoir they were able to harness the water to generate hydro-electric power. It was in 1920, thanks to Shiro Koga, that electricity replaced the oil lamps on Bowen Island. Next, he constructed a long system of pipes supplying clean, fresh drinking water to the hotel and also to the camping grounds. Later a sewage removal system was constructed. In addition, under his supervision, the Japanese workers operated the farm which produced dairy cattle, poultry, and hogs as well as fresh fruit and vegetables. Transporting guests to and from the resort; transporting huge cargoes of food stuffs and construction materials, and providing the services required for the summer resort were his responsibility.

One of his masterpieces of construction was the oriental style wooden bridge, painted red, which arched majestically over a pretty waterfall. Below the bridge he built a serene pond with water fowl swimming to and fro. On the shore of the pond stood a beautiful red-roofed cottage, around which was a Japanese garden. From the bridge ran a long winding romantic walk which people called Lover's Lane. Man and nature surely met here.

Eventually, he was freed from family obligations and began to think of settling down, so with his small capital he started a sawmill and in a year or so saved enough money to buy fifteen acres of uncleared land at Port Haney. His aim was to become an independent landowner farmer. He toiled day and night clearing the land with hand and pick — in a most primitive way — but he turned this piece of land into a productive strawberry farm. He then built a cozy home right in the middle of his farm land, and married a very attractive woman named Mon. Her love and devotion to him were indeed his everlasting good fortune for they prospered and were blessed with a beautiful daughter and two sons. His success as a strawberry farmer attracted other Japanese pioneers to start farming in Port Haney, B.C.

Japanese strawberry farmers grew in numbers and they soon realized that it was necessary to organize a growers' association in order to expand into the profitable produce market. The Growers' Association was established and a system of quality control of the strawberry crop was established. In order to prevent flooding the market with their crops it was sometimes necessary to hold the cargo in storage for a time. A method of packing and crating the strawberries was standardized. Information concerning new and better varieties of strawberry plants, fertilizers, insect control, etc., were given to the members of the association. The association was able to buy large quantities of fertilizers, crates, insecticides, etc., and thus sell these to the members at reasonable costs.

Soon it was necessary to have a meeting place, so a hall was built. The hall was used for other purposes such as Japanese and English language schools, a kindergarten, and on Sundays, a Church.

Shiro Koga was elected president of the association and through his leadership the foundation was laid for co-operatively developing the berry industry and marketing their produce which would be beneficial for all member growers in the Port Haney area.

The Koga family, like other Japanese were forced to relocate. They left their beloved farm land for a sugar beet farm near Winnipeg, Manitoba, where the temperature dropped to thirty degrees below zero in winter. The work on the beet farm must have been extremely hard for him, especially with three young children and a wife to feed on a meagre salary. When his morale was at the lowest, he met Rev. Yoshimitsu Akagawa, a noted United Church minister, who inspired him to accept life as a Christian and so he became a strong and faithful member of the church. When he was dying he said to family and friends, "I am the happiest man in the world. God is inviting me to come. I am ready to go." So saying, Shiro Koga passed away without pain or sorrow on October 22, 1974 and joined his wife who had died in 1957.

Anno Makishi and Seiku Sakumoto
Pioneers From Okinawa

In the years 1906 and 1907 the Canadian Pacific Railway was in the midst of constructing its railroad and needed many labourers. Nikka Yotatsu'Sha (The Japan-Canada Supply Co.) was an agency set up to bring Japanese workers for this project and advertised for immigrants widely in Japan. Among the more than 1,200 immigrants who came were 153 men from Okinawa prefecture. Since seventy-five years have gone by only two of the original 153 survive; Mr. Kyosei Kohashigawa, ninety-three, is living at Lethbridge, Alberta and Mr. Tokusuke Oyakawa, ninety-four, resides in Nipigon, Ontario.

There were two other men from Okinawa who had arrived in Victoria three years before the main immigration — Mr. Anno Makishi and Mr. Oyadomari came to Canada in 1903. Mr. Oyadomari stayed in Canada for about seventeen years and then went back to his native prefecture, Okinawa but Mr. Makishi stayed on thus becoming the first Okinawan-Canadian pioneer. Mr. Makishi was employed by the C.P.R. at Kenora, Ontario for a while, then in 1918 moved to Lyalta, Alberta where he purchased a farm. In 1940, he and his family moved to Picture Butte and then to Coaldale, Alberta in 1941, where they farmed, growing vegetables and raising pigs. He was born of a samurai family and was educated primarily in the Chinese Confucianist school. He was a real gentleman, dignified, deeply honourable, and kindly to the newly arrived Okinawan immigrants. He was respected not only by his own countrymen but also by occidental neighbours. I met him right after I arrived in Coaldale, Alberta from Slocan City in 1945. Mr. Makishi converted and became a very faithful member of the Church of the Ascension in Coaldale. His family consisted of his wife Kiyo, daughter Mary, and son Edward. When Mr. Makishi died in 1965, I officiated at his funeral service.

I would like to introduce another outstanding Okinawan pioneer by the name of Mr. Seiku Sakumoto.

I met Mr. Sakumoto for the first time in 1920 when I was attending an English Language class at the Powell Street Japanese Methodist night school. Twenty five years later we met again in Southern Alberta. Since then we have maintained our fellowship.

"Mr. Sakumoto, please tell me when and where you were born," I asked one day in April, 1982 when I visited him and his wife.

"I was born December, 1900 at Yomitan, Okinawa," he replied.

When he was fifteen he arrived in Vancouver, B.C. He was sponsored by his father, Seiko, who came to Canada in 1907 with the original 153 Okinawan people. Seiko Sakumoto was working with his fellow C.P.R. labourers at Kenora, Ontario after having previously worked on a farm in B.C. At one time he had operated a grocery store in Vancouver. Unfortunately the work in Kenora was too hard for him and he passed away with a heart attack six months before his son Seiku arrived. How sad and lonely Seiku must have felt. Fortunately his older brother Taro was already living in Vancouver so they went to Kenora together and worked there for three years. Taro married in 1919 and has a daughter, Hiroko. (Hiroko married the late James Tamagi. The Tamagi story is elsewhere in this collection.) The Sakumotos found the winters in Kenora severe and as they did not have many friends there, they moved back to Vancouver in 1920 to re-establish themselves.

At that time Mr. Taro Takeyasu, who was the foreman of the shingle mill called the Pearson and Anderson Shingle Co., hired the two brothers. Seiku decided to continue his studies but it was not an easy matter to study English at night school after ten hours of hard work at the mill. However, he kept on studying for three years and finally entered King George High School at twenty-two years of age. There were four other Japanese students at that school — Satoru Chiya, Katsumi Takahashi, Toyoji Yasuda, and Sakaru Saita.

(Takahashi was a nephew of Dr. Takahashi of Vancouver.) They graduated from school in 1925 and the four entered university that fall. Seiku entered Pre-med School of Pharmacy and Science and completed the college course in one year. He wanted to go on to university, but found it difficult to further his studies.

About this time his brother Taro's wife passed away leaving three little children, Sam, Hiroko, and Mary, the latter just a baby who was born weak. Both Sam and Mary died young — Mary at seventeen in 1940 on Christmas day and Sam at twenty-two in 1943. Before Mrs. Taro Sakumoto died, she begged Seiku to marry her niece, Teru, who was still in Okinawa, and also she asked him to help Taro raise her three children.

"When we married in 1923, he was still a student," Mrs. Sakumoto said.

At that time it was difficult to call a bride from Japan. With the help of Rev. Yoshimitsu Akagawa, Rev. Dr. Osterhout, and Mr. Yataro Arikado, who was the President of the Japanese Association, Mr. Sakumoto was able to send for Teru without trouble.

"I wanted to go on to study medicine at university but there was no medical course at the University of British Columbia. To go to another university in a far distant city was impossible because of the extraordinary expense. Mr. Saita, (later Dr. Saita) who was studying at Wisconsin University Medical School, urged me to join him but I could not do so as I was now responsible for my wife and my brother's children," he said with a deep sigh.

Needing a job, Mr. Sakumoto went to the office of the *Minshu Daily Newspaper (The People's Daily Newspaper)*, the official organ of the Camp and Labour Local 31, to see Mr. Tokue Kameoka, the manager of the paper. Mr. Etsuji Suzuki, the editor of the *Minshu Daily* asked Mr. Sakumoto to work for the Japanese Labour Union and be spokesman for the Union at the Labour Federation of Vancouver. He was to assist Mr. Suzuki also in the Labour Union movement among Japanese Canadians. They agreed he be paid $75 a month and Seiku began to work for the union. He worked in this position for two years and attended Labour Federation meetings twice a month.

Mr. Suzuki started writing editorials criticizing the Japanese Association, the Japanese Canadian Merchants' Association and the Japanese merchants for grasping excessive profits. The result was the withdrawl of subscriptions and advertisements from the *Minshu Daily Newspaper.* In order to compete with the merchants, the Minshu Kobai Kumiai (The People's Co-Operative) was organized and Mr. Sakumoto began to work in this new Co-Operative with Mr. Iwashita of Kelowna. Within a short period of time they gathered about 1,000 members. He worked for this organization as a book-keeper until 1930 for a monthly wage of $75.

In the mean time Mr. and Mrs. Sakumoto were blessed with their own two children. He found it difficult to manage with only $75 a month so he left the job and began to sell wood and coal. At first he only used one truck but in a few years the business prospered requiring three big trucks to deliver the fuel. As his business was thriving he was able to send his wife, daughter, and niece to visit Japan in 1936.

When the Imperial Japanese Air Force attacked Pearl Harbour, the Japanese Canadians were dragged into the Second World War. The R.C.M.P. came and ordered Mr. Sakumoto to go to a road camp to help build a highway in the Rocky Mountains. But he was also advised that if he would leave the 100 miles restricted coastal area within 24 hours he would be allowed to do so. Immediately, he handed his business over to his nephew, Sam, who was a Nisei, thinking that his nephew could carry on the business. He left Vancouver, and went to Yale, B.C., a town near Hope, as that place was outside the restricted area. When he arrived at Yale, the anti-Japanese sentiment here was so strong that he could not get a room nor was he able to eat at a restaurant which refused to serve him.

He telephoned his family in Vancouver and left for Calgary, Alberta hoping to contact Mr. Eiro Nago, his friend who was a hotel bell boy. When he met Mr. Nago, he discovered Mr. Nago too was out of work because he was Japanese. Seiku set off once more searching for a refuge. On the train he met Mr. Edamura, who was also fleeing from Vancouver. These two evacuees travelled together to Lethbridge, Alberta.

Fortunately at the Lethbridge railway station they met Mr. Bokushin Kanashiro, another fellow Okinawan, who previously settled in Lethbridge. Mr. Kanashiro took Mr. Sakumoto and Mr. Edamura to the Medoruma's farm in Iron Springs. When they asked for shelter they learned that Mr. Medoruma was helping another Japanese family called Maruyama, so there was no room for them. If was off season for chickens, so they cleaned the small chicken house and lived there for a month and a half. Seiku sent for his family and his brother Taro's family and they worked together at Scott's farm in Iron Springs for a number of years before opening a store in Lethbridge. The business thrived, and he served his community well before retiring to Vancouver, B.C. Mr. and Mrs. Seiku Sakumoto's son, Dr. George Sakumoto, a dentist, resides in Richmond, B.C., the second son, an architect, lives in Edmonton, Alberta, and daughter, Amy Higa, lives with her dentist husband at West Vancouver, B.C.

Seiku Sakumoto, a well known and respected Japanese Canadian pioneer, helped many Okinawan immigrants as well as other Japanese Canadians for many years.

George Kiyozo Kaguta, 1978

Kiyozo Kazuta
Who Contributed Much for
the Welfare of the Japanese in Canada

Kiyozo Kazuta, the youngest of four sons, was born 1899, at Hiroshima, Japan, where he attended primary, secondary and technical continuation schools. Called by his elder brother, he arrived in Victoria, B.C. on January 5, 1917. The following day he came to Vancouver and found employment with an occidental family as a school boy in order to learn English. He found learning to speak English was not an easy matter. He was receiving $5 per month plus room and board while his friend, Katsutaro Hayashi, who was also a school boy, was only being paid $4 a month and had to do the laundry as well. Katsutaro too was having problems learning English. One day, when he was washing clothes in the basement, the master of the house called Katsutaro and said, "Dena". Katsutaro was shocked and could not understand what he was doing wrong, being ordered in this very crude and rough way to dena, or 'get out and get lost'. Well, Katsutaro soon found out that it wasn't 'dena' but 'dinner time'.

After being a school boy for two months, Kiyozo Kazuta found work at the Hastings sawmill earning $1.75 per day for ten hours of work. He was always trying to learn English from every Japanese mission in the city — the Roman Catholics, the Anglicans, and the Methodists. When he learned some English he got a job with the Kelly Douglas Company in order to learn business practices. However, his English was not good enough so he decided to go to school. They would not let him into Lord Robert School at English Bay but he finally managed, at age twenty, to be admitted to grade three at Dawson School. It wasn't hard being at the top of the class in all subjects except in English. Later he entered a business school. The school fees were twenty-two dollars per month. In order to pay for the fees, he and his friend worked as night janitors for forty-five dollars a month and divided these wages equally between them. As they needed more money to pay for lodging and food, they worked at a

171

bowling alley for thirty cents an hour. It was not easy work.

After graduating from business college, he worked for the Kagetsu Company for ten years. This company was one of the largest logging establishments within the Japanese Canadian community at that time. During this period, there was a strong anti-Japanese sentiment in B.C., also a severe economic depression all over the world which affected the Japanese in B.C. in the fishing, lumbering and farming industries.

In 1937, Kazuta married and left the Kagetsu Company and started his own grocery store in Vancouver. After several years in the business, he sold the store and worked first for the *Nichi Nichi* newspaper, then the Strawberry Hill Japanese Farmers' Union and finally a Chinese company called the Dan, which engaged in the wholesale vegetable trade.

The Pacific War started on December 7, 1941, and he was advised to appear at the evacuation office on February 17, 1942, where there were many Japanese being examined by a doctor. After the examination they were ordered to go to a road camp that night. This order was really very cruel for the men had only one afternoon to make preparations to leave their wives, children, homes and businesses. When lunch hour came, some of them wanted to go home for a meal and others wanted to make some kind of business arrangements. When one of the men said he wanted to go home for a meal, a Japanese who was handling the case said, "You have eaten a regular meal (komeno meshi) for thirty or forty years, so you can omit today's."

Had there been no R.C.M.P. officer in the office, there would have been a great deal of trouble.

Mr. Kazuta went home for lunch and then went shopping. At about 3:00 p.m. he went back to the evacuation office, but there were no evacuees there. An officer asked, "Why didn't you come earlier? Everybody left for the road camp already."

"You did not tell me what time to be back so I went shopping," Kazuta replied.

"It is too late. Come back tomorrow morning," the officer ordered. So Mr. Kazuta went to the office early the next morning and was sent to Lempriere, B.C., which is near the Alberta-B.C. border. He spent two months in this terribly cold and snowy place and one day was called back to Vancouver as his wife had applied to go to a sugar beet farm where they would be allowed to live together as a family. However, when he returned he found that another family had been placed on that farm. So they had to wait for the next opening. Finally on August 22, 1942, he was advised to enter Hastings Park and was questioned as to whether or not he was willing to go east. He was also told that if he was not willing to go he would have to go to an internment camp.

Mr. Kazuta was given a job at Hastings Park Manning Centre, earning fifteen cents an hour. The morale was very low here; teenagers were wild, thieves many. He had to leave his family but was allowed to visit them and was given a pass. His job was to look after the public baths and he worked there until his family was sent to Tashme. They arrived at Tashme on October 27, 1942. Kiyozo was chosen as one of the committee members of the Japanese Canadian Association and served on the welfare committee.

In order to find out what sort of experience he had before the Second World War, I asked, "Please tell about some important experiences that you would like to tell the Japanese Canadians."

"Before the Second World War the first generation of Japanese in Canada had to face terrible anti-Japanese feelings in B.C. The first anti-Japanese movement was seen in the persecution of the Japanese Canadian fishermen with the decreasing of the number of licences issued to them. Because of the reduction of licences issued, most of the unlicenced fishermen were put out of work. This anti-Japanese fishermen's law was introduced by an M.P. from the west coast of Vancouver Island with the full support of the white fishermen's union.

"There were quite a number of small business establishments in Vancouver such as the corner grocery stores which suffered. Around Christmas time, boxes of Japanese mandarin oranges were delivered to the Vancouver stores for sale. One time we sold a box to a boy who came to buy it in the afternoon, and later the boy's father returned the box of oranges saying that the Japanese were using the money earned from the sales to manufacture bombs to kill the Chinese.

"In 1928, the Vancouver Japanese School Board wanted to build their own school but because they feared anti-Japanese sentiment, they called the building the 'Japanese Hall'.

"The thirty-three Japanese Canadian veterans who fought for Canada during the First World War and who were living in Vancouver about that time did not have the right to vote. They appealed to the B.C. government for the franchise and the decision was passed in their favour with just one or two dissenting votes.

"With regards to the lumber industry, there was a law in B.C. that restricted the Japanese from working on government lands. Those who were engaged in the lumber industry such as Mr. Eikichi Kagetsu, Mr. Kaminishi and others suffered by the restrictions. There was a member of parliament who was a champion of anti-Japanese discrimination. And as we Japanese did not have the right to vote in those days, we were placed in a very difficult position.

"There were three fishing districts in which the Japanese fishermen could fish, the Fraser River and around the inland sea; Vancouver Island and the west coast, and the Skeena and Nass Rivers and the sea around. They could not fish outside their fishing areas, while the others could fish anywhere. As well the white fishermen could use gasoline powered boats while the Japanese could not. It must have been hard to fish around the Skeena River such as at Sunnyside, Port Edwards and Claxton areas where the river runs very fast. I want to tell you of an episode that happened with regards to the practice of restricting the use of gasoline powered boats. There was a highly educated man by the name of Mr. Jun Kizawa, who was a fisherman and the secretary of the Japanese Fishermen's Association in the Skeena River district. He was born at Hashimoto City, Wakayama-ken, Japan and after graduating from Waseda University in Tokyo, he came to Canada and became a fisherman. One day he wilfully got an old gasoline powered boat and went out fishing. He got caught and he eloquently defended the right of all citizens to fair play and equal treatment just like a preacher, preaching about God's justice. Consequently, the Japanese fishermen were allowed to use gasoline powered boats.

"I think the Japanese Canadians who suffered most due to the Second World War were the farmers along the Fraser River, such as Haney, Hammond, Mission, Surrey, etc. Unless you worked clearing the thick, tangled forest you cannot understand the untold hardships the farmers endured clearing the land by hand and horse power. To uproot big trees, some as big as ten feet in diameter was not an easy task. Sometimes dynamite was used and that was very dangerous and bad accidents occurred. One such happened in Surrey. When a neighbour of the Ujiye's was clearing land, he lit the dynamite to remove a big stump. Because it did not explode in a specified time, he went to see what was wrong. When he was almost a foot away from the stump, there was an explosion and he was killed instantly. Such was the hard life of the Japanese farmers but they were rewarded as the land began to bear fruit. But suddenly with the coming of the Pacific War the Government of Canada removed the Japanese Canadians. Great injustice was done. The communities established before the war, under the most trying conditions were destroyed and were not allowed to re-establish. As you well know the government did not relocate the Germans, Italians and other ethnics.

"Now times have changed and I think it is difficult for

the younger generation of Japanese Canadians and the new immigrants from Japan to comprehend the great hardships and deprivation we Issei pioneers suffered in our early years in Canada. That we endured to establish for our future generations a place in Canadian life is something worth while remembering. We old Isseis hope that the coming generations will remember us for our industriousness, endurance and courage.''

Katsuyoshi Morita
and the Japanese Canadian
Industrial Business Men's Club

I would like to introduce Mr. Katsuyoshi Morita who now resides in Vancouver, B.C., and who knows the origin of the Nippon Jitsugyo Club (the Japanese Canadian Industrial and Business Men's Club).

Katsuyoshi Morita was born September 5, 1899 at Iyomishima, Ehime-ken, Japan, and was the eldest son of Mr. Sanji Morita and his wife, Matsuyo. His father passed away when Katsuyoshi was nine years old and at age eleven he went to the city of Osaka in order to learn to become a good Japanese cook. He spent nine years in training and at the end of the training period he was made the chief cook of a restaurant.

Recently when I met him I asked him why he decided to emigrate and why he chose Canada. He replied, "While I was working at a famous Japanese restaurant in Osaka a gentleman, by the name of Rikimatsu Tabata, an exporter of salted Canadian salmon, used to visit his father who lived near where I lived. He came almost every year from Canada after the salmon season was over and he told us much about this beautiful country and especially about Vancouver, B.C. That's why I wanted to come here."

Katsuyoshi Morita arrived at Vancouver in 1917. Anti-Japanese sentiments were high and the Consul of Japan, the Honourable Goji Ukita, felt the need of organizing a club to discuss and to find some way of stopping the anti-Japanese movement. He called a meeting of prominent business and industrial people to organize a club and the following were established as the objectives of the club: 1. To promote good relationships between Canada and Japan. 2. To promote better relationships between the members of the club for the betterment of the Japanese in Canada. 3. To find ways and means of combatting anti-Japanese movements.

It was felt that the above objectives would meet the needs of the Japanese Canadians at that time and the club was organized March 3, 1920. Its office was on the third floor of Mr. Rikimatsu Tabata's building at 362 Alexander St., Vancouver, B.C. The second floor of the building was used as a restaurant and the proprietor of the restaurant was Mr. Chonosuke Wakano, a brother-in-law of Mr. Tabata. Mr. Morita agreed to work in this restaurant as the chief cook for a period of three years. Japanese waitresses, were hired who were trained in the art of Japanese music such as playing the samisen, and in Japanese dance, such as the Tokiwaza and Gidayu. In all, they had two Japanese girls who entertained and two others who served customers. Many merchant seamen, sailors and train travellers came to the restaurant to relax after a long journey, to eat the excellent fresh fish cooked by Mr. Morita and to enjoy the nostalgia of Japanese music and songs and dances. Of course the members of the club often took their meals at this restaurant too.

After serving his agreed on three years, he returned to Japan and married Tsuruno in 1924. They arrived at Vancouver in the same year, bought the restaurant and carried on business until 1930.

As far as Mr. Katsuyoshi Morita remembers the officers and committee members of the Japanese Canadian Industrial and Business Men's Club were as follows: The Advisor: The Honourable Goji Ukita, the Consul of Japan, The President: Mr. Saori Goto. Committee Members:

Katsuyoshi Morita , 1920

Messrs. Matsunoshin Abe, Sumio Tateishi, Japanese Canadian Association representatives; Messrs. Genichi Kodama, Teiichi Noritaka, Bank representatives; Mr. Sataro Fujita, Kinyusha Trust Co., representative; Dr. Neinosuke Ishiwara, M.D.; Dr. Abe, Dr. Tai Kuzuhara, Dentists; Mr. Yasushi Yamazaki, Publisher of the Continental Times; Mr. Chokotsu Ishii, of the Canada *Nichi Nichi* Newspaper; Messrs. Ichiro Yamamoto, Saori Goto, Nikka Yotatsu agents; Messrs. Sotojiro Matsumiya, Sentaro Uchida, Tahei Niimi, and the Tanabe brothers, Japanese Businessmen representatives; Mr. Tetsuzo Matsumato, Ship builder; Messrs. Rikimatsu Tabata, Takejiro Oode, Jukichi Korenaga, Sankichi Tanaka, Fishery representatives; Messrs. Mosaburo Oda, Kunimatsu Saimoto, Steveston Fishery representatives; Messrs. Eikichi Kagetsu, Kenroku Uchiyama. Sho Kiminishi, Forestry representatives; Messrs. Kaoru Tanaka, Mohei Sato, Hyakutaro Honda, Hotel owner's representatives.

The membership of the club rose to one hundred at this time. There were other organizations such as the dry cleaners, restaurants, barbers associations but Mr. Morita does not remember that any representatives from these organizations were present. The Jitsugyo Club functioned until 1935 or 1936 when it was taken over by Mr. Etsuji Morii and his group and the name of this club was changed to the 'Nippon Club'. When the Pacific War started in 1941, the Nippon Club struck a new committee called the Morii Committee which dealt with the total evacuation of Japanese Canadians from the protected coastal area.

"After Japan attacked Pearl Harbour," Mr. Morita said, "I received a notice as did all Japanese male Nationals, aged eighteen to fifty-five, ordering me to go to the road camp in the interior of B.C. The notice contained the following sentence: 'To all Japanese National males; You came to Canada with just a cloth bag from Japan. We must endure even though our possessions are taken away from us. The order of the government is very important. Please obey the orders of the Canadian government until the war is ended . . .'

179

"I told my wife and children that there were incidents in Siberia and Northern China where a group of Japanese soldiers massacred the Russian and Chinese people. So in order to avoid trouble, we must obey the governmental order and the family must behave calmly while I am away at the road camp. If we obey the law, the Canadian government will protect us."

However, Mr. Morita was not sent to a road camp due to poor health and instead he, his wife and five children were relocated to Greenwood, B.C., one of the five ghost town camps in the interior of B.C.

Mr. and Mrs. Katsuyoshi Morita celebrated their golden wedding anniversary in 1974, and were looking forward to their diamond anniversary. But sadly, Mrs. Morita passed away in September, 1981. Mr. Morita, now retired, lives with one of his daughters. Loved by his children and ten grandchildren, he spends his retirement years tending the flower garden which his wife loved.

Hanako Sato and Tsutae Sato C.M.
Educators

In March, 1982 I visited two outstanding pioneers in the field of education — Tsutae and Hanako Sato of Vancouver, B.C. For several decades these dedicated teachers were the instrumental forces guiding the development of the Japanese Language School system in Canada.

Born and raised in Tanamura machi, Fukushima-ken in 1891, Mr. Sato attended the primary school of the village, followed by studies in Chinese classics at a private school. Then a short term Normal School opened and he continued his education there. After graduating at the age of sixteen he found employment as a teacher at a local primary school. He only taught at this school for one year as he decided to pursue his own academic career by enrolling at Aoyama Normal College in Tokyo where he studied for five years. After graduation, he again worked as a teacher, this time at Shibuya Primary School for four years. While teaching there he received an invitation from the Vancouver Japanese Language School which he accepted and arrived in Vancouver in 1917.

Mr. Sato's wife, Hanako, was born in Wakayama-ken, but moved to Tokyo when she was only a year old. Then the family moved to Niigata when she was about kindergarten age, and a few years later to Toyama. Because her father was a medical doctor, the family was forced to move from one city to another as he was frequently relocated. Finally, however, the family settled down in Tokyo. Like Mr. Sato, Hanako was a graduate of Aoyama Normal College and came to Canada as a teacher on the invitation of the Japanese Language School of Vancouver, four years after Mr. Sato arrived as a principal.

"What was the condition of the Japanese Language School at the time you took over the principalship?" I asked Mr. Sato.

"The name of the school was Nippon Kokumin Gakko (Japanese National School). At that time most parents were working hard to gain enough money to return to Japan. The parents wanted to educate their children exactly as the Japanese schools in Japan were doing using Japanese textbooks in all subjects, and attending from morning to late afternoon so that their children could experience the same education as the children in Japan."

The Vancouver Kokumin Gakko started in 1906 and lasted until 1922. Then the school began to teach English in addition to Japanese. The first principal of this Kokumin Gakko was Mr. Kozuka, who held the post for one year. Mr. Torao Tanaka followed him and then four or five years later the principal of the school was Mr. Katsunosuke Tashiro. He was a strong willed principal and during this time "Ijikai" (the supporting association of the school) was organized.

Mr. Shigejiro Inouye followed Mr. Tashiro. He did not stay at the school for very long, as his salary was not sufficient to support his large family. Later he became involved in a Japanese silk importing business and opened a successful store in Edmonton.

Tsutae Sato followed Mr. Shigejiro Inouye as the fifth principal of the Vancouver Japanese Language School in 1917. Four years later his future wife, Hanako came to Canada as a teacher of this school. She was single then, but she had become acquainted with Mr. Sato in Tokyo when he was teaching her younger brother at Shibuya Public School. She came to Canada with the understanding that she and Mr. Sato would be married. Their wedding took place shortly after her arrival in Vancouver.

There were about 150 students registered at the Vancouver school when Mr. Sato took over as principal, but the enrollment rapidly increased, especially after 1936 and it reached over 1,000 when the school closed in 1942 due to the evacuation.

As mentioned previously, the majority of the Japanese immigrants hoped to go back to Japan. Unfortunately, however, most of them could not make enough money and as the number of children increased, new responsibilities and expenses were added to the burden. Eventually, the dream slipped further and further from their reach. When they made the decision to remain in Canada, they realized that their Canadian children needed to be educated as Canadians and with the exception of a very few, most children were sent to Canadian public schools. At the same time, the anti-Japanese movement became very strong in British Columbia and the Japanese school was accused of being the centre of Japanese nationalism. In order to avoid any confrontations with anti-Japanese groups, the administrators of the school decided to make some major changes in the school system.

Mr. Sato urged the parents to send their children to Canadian public schools during the day, and by 1923 there was not one Kokumin Gakko student left in the Japanese school. Japanese education became of secondary importance, taking place after regular school hours.

In short, the evolution of the Vancouver Japanese Language School was as follows: strictly Japanese education from 1906 to 1911; then mainly Japanese education in addition to English instruction at the Japanese Language School; and finally, public school education in Canadian schools with the teaching of Japanese confined to no more than two hours after public school hours.

If there had been no Japanese school in existence some of the parents would have sent their children to Japan for an education. This would have entailed extra money, and widened the gap between parents and children, resulting in general family disunity.

Another important role served by the Japanese Language School was the facilitating of adult education among the parents of the students through Ijikai, Parent-Teacher associations, Mothers' associations, etc. There existed a desire to promote understanding between the Japanese and non-Japanese communities in Canada. One time, for example, the school held a fund raising drive to send a Canadian teacher from Strathcona Public School to Japan.

The successful development of the school can be largely attributed to Mr. and Mrs. Sato. For several decades they worked on upgrading and improving the quality of education offered by the school. And they were the ones primarily responsible for the establishment of the Japanese Canadian Language Schools Federation, as well as for the addition of a larger school building.

The Japanese Language Schools Federation functioned until 1941 when the Pacific War broke out. It fostered a peaceful and harmonious relationship between Japanese schools, thus strengthening the Japanese community as a whole. The main school building in Vancouver was in itself a kind of focal point for the community, as the school auditorium was often used for community meetings because of the lack of a formal Japanese community hall. Even today, the school still serves this purpose.

The evacuation from the B.C. coast brought a sudden end to the schools, which up until then had been prospering with increased enrollments every year. Mr. and Mrs. Sato spent eleven years at Lacombe, Alberta, from 1942 to 1953.

During this time they managed to travel to practically all the places where their former students resettled in order to comfort and encourage them.

"We were asked to go to Toronto and start a Japanese school there," states Mr. Sato. "But we preferred to re-establish our school in Vancouver so returned here in 1953. Today there are many Japanese schools in Canada but there is no school which has its own school building, except ours."

Times have changed, and the aims and ideals of the Japanese Language School have changed too. The children who attend these language schools now are the sons and daughters of second and third generation Japanese Canadians. They speak English throughout the day, at home and at public school. And most of them do not understand why they have to study Japanese.

The influence of the Satos is deeply felt by many Japanese Canadians, especially the older Nisei. In their retirement years, the Satos were comforted by visits and letters from their former students.

Mr. Sato's contribution to the Japanese Canadian community was recognized by the Canadian government in 1980 when he was named a member of the Order of Canada.

"It is indeed a great honour for us," remarked Mr. Sato, when I interviewed him. "We do not know who recommended us and how this came about. We feel we have fulfilled our life's work."

"Was there any special time when you worried or experienced difficulties?" I asked.

"Yes. When we built our school I worried, as we did not have enough money to start it. And just about when the Second World War started the city council passed anti-Japanese school regulations, and it was very difficult for us to carry on. The reason for this anti-Japanese school legislation was that we were using text books published in Japan for Japanese children. The Vancouver city officials became very agitated, claiming that we were teaching Japanese militarism."

The Satos endured many hard times, but they looked

back on their days of trial with joy and gladness, as they saw the results of their work. Most graduates of their school were doing very well, among them university professors, medical doctors, successful businessmen, journalists, bankers, etc. There are also some Christian ministers such as Rev. Takatami, Rev. Tomita and Rev. Matsuga. The Satos' hope and desire was to educate children to be good Canadian citizens and to contribute to the welfare of both Canada and Japan. Fulfilling this dream for them are people such as Mr. Shinobu Higashi of Kyodo Press of Japan and Mr. Kazuma Nakayama who served as a foreign affairs secretary of Japan.

I left the Satos' home with a deep sense of admiration and respect for these two dedicated teachers who laboured for the betterment of Japanese Canadians. The fruits of their efforts can certainly be witnessed today.

Mrs. Sato passed away in May 1983 and Mr. Sato died days later.

What I Remember about Takaichi Umezuki C.M.

Throughout my long life I have known many people and one of my personal friends about whom I have happy memories is the late Mr. Takaichi Umezuki.

I met him for the first time in the winter of 1919 when he was a student at the English night school of Vancouver Japanese Methodist Church 500 Powell St., Vancouver. He was a very studious and a rather quiet person, I thought. As we were both young and had many other activities we did not have much contact. He told me he was two years older than I was, so he must have been born in 1898. His native place was Fukuoka-ken.

I am not sure when he came to Canada but I believe it was one or two years before I did — that is 1917 or 1918. I know he came to work at the printing department of the *Tairiku Nippo (The Continental Daily News)* where Mr. Etsu Suzuki was the editor-in-chief.

My closer friendship with him began in the summer of 1922 at Port Haney, B.C. In 1976, when I was planning a third trip to South America, he wrote an article in *The New Canadian* in which he described the close relationship we had as young men.

"It was the summer of 1922" he wrote, "when Goichi Nakayama and I spent our days picking strawberries at Mr. Jiro Inouye's farm in Haney. We lived together in a small farm house in the pasture with Mr. Yoshida, a young immigrant from Japan who was called by Mr. Inouye. I went to Haney to learn farming as Mr. and Mrs. Etsu Suzuki and myself were contemplating establishing our ideal of living communally in the country.

"On the other side of the Trunk Road Highway, lived Mr. and Mrs. Ryoji and even now Mrs. Setsuko Ryoji teases me saying; 'A young man trying to learn how to farm and holding a book in one hand? That young man was you, Mr. Umezuki.' I do not know if this description fits me or not, but after I left Mr. Inouye's farm I moved to the farm of an easy going carpenter-farmer, Mr. Hainz. I lived there for two years, enjoying life, working on sunny days and reading many books on rainy days."

Through the leadership of Mr. Etsu Suzuki, the Japanese Canadian Labour Union was established and a weekly newspaper was published. As membership increased there was a need for a daily newspaper. So Mr. Suzuki left the *Tairiku Nippo* and became the editor of *The Minshu — The People's Daily Newspaper*. Mr. Umezuki joined *The Minshu* and he worked very hard in the printing department of the paper. The paper would never have existed without Mr. Umezuki, since he was our only experienced printer. Mr. Furukawa helped him for a while but he left for Japan leaving Mr. Umezuki alone. This newspaper started in 1923.

Mr. Umezuki lived with Mr. and Mrs. Etsu Suzuki and was greatly influenced by their ideals and dedication to the labour movement.

By this time the Nisei were maturing and there was need of an English newspaper — so Mr. Thomas Shoyama,

Mr. Edward Ouchi, Mr. Shinobu Higashi, etc. started an English newspaper called *The New Canadian*.

The Second World War started and the Canadian government forced the closing of all Japanese newspapers and Japanese language schools. However, *The New Canadian* was allowed to publish and was closely censored by the B.C. Security Commission. Later the authorities realized the need of Japanese sections in the newspaper and Mr. Umezuki, formerly of *The Minshu* joined *The New Canadian* as Japanese editor and later became publisher of *The New Canadian*.

During the war years, *The New Canadian* was moved to Kaslo, B.C., one of the internment camps. After that the paper was published in Winnipeg for awhile and later it was moved to Toronto where it is still being published.

Mr. Takaichi Umezuki proved to be a leader for all the Japanese Canadian communities through his editorials in *The New Canadian*. His direct and sharp warnings or criticisms of his fellow Japanese Canadians sometimes caused misunderstandings and resentment, but he bravely kept on without compromising or wavering, and usually he was right. He was greatly respected and loved by his associates as well as his many friends.

One day in 1976 I visited him at his office in Toronto on my way home from my trip to South America.

"How are you?" I inquired.

"Not so well," he answered "I am having problems of aging."

We were both very health conscious and spent a long time discussing diet, exercise and health cures about which I had recently learned. The articles on health were of help especially to elderly Issei.

Unfortunately, his loving wife passed away very suddenly. He remarried in 1971 and had surgery for brain tumor in 1978. He recovered somewhat and was able to work a little. In 1979 he was honoured by the Canadian government and was made a member of the Order of Canada. On January 23, 1980, he passed away suddenly at the age of eighty-two years.

My brief sketch does not do justice to this outstanding Japanese Canadian but I am glad to hear that a book in his honour is being created, which will provide more details.

Mr. and Mrs. Z. Shimbashi
A Couple who Served the Prince of Wales

I met Zenkichi and Teru Shimbashi right after the Second World War, when I went to Coaldale, Alberta, to establish an Anglican Japanese Mission. At that time they were engaged in sugar beet farming in Raymond, Alberta. In their lifetime they experienced a rare opportunity of meeting and serving the Prince of Wales, who later became King Edward VIII of England.

About twenty-eight miles south west of the city of Calgary, there is a town called High River. Near this town, in the foothills of the beautiful Canadian Rocky Mountains there are many cattle ranches, and the most famous one is the E. P. Ranch. It was famous because the owner of this ranch was the Prince of Wales of England. We do not know for what reasons he spent five summers here from 1923 to 1928. Perhaps he was of a liberal mind and wished freedom away from the strict traditional royal life in England, which later forced him to abdicate his throne in order to marry Mrs. Wallace Simpson, a woman of his choice and an American divorcee. The Prince of Wales came to the E. P. Ranch for the first time when he was about twenty-four years of age.

One day Mr. and Mrs. Shimbashi were reading a newspaper and they saw an advertisement for a cook for the E. P. Ranch. They applied for the position and were accepted. They moved to the ranch and worked as cooks for five years. Zenkichi Shimbashi came to Canada when he was sixteen years old and this incident happened ten years after he landed in Canada.

To serve as a cook for a member of the Royal family of England in Canada is unusual, especially for a Japanese

Canadian. While the Shimbashis were working at the E. P. Ranch, their first son was born and they named him Edward in honour of their master, Edward, the Prince of Wales. They left the ranch when the Prince's ranch was transferred to other owners.

It was about Christmas time in 1928 when the Shimbashis received a parcel from His Royal Highness, the King of England. They were overjoyed to be remembered and when they opened the parcel they found a lovely night gown for Mrs. Shimbashi and a handsome watch for Mr. Shimbashi. For many years they exchanged greetings with the King.

They remembered the Prince of Wales pouring his own coffee or tea even though there were many attendants about. They witnessed the Prince acting as if he was just a common man, mixing freely with ordinary people.

Mr. Shimbashi was born in Kokubu, Kagoshima-ken in 1897. After coming to Canada he worked for a few years in B.C. but finding the work physically very hard and the wages meagre because of the anti-oriental attitudes in B.C., he went to Alberta in 1917 when he was 20 years old. He found the people in Alberta friendlier and believed that Alberta offered a better future for him so he decided to remain there. A few years later he became a naturalized Canadian citizen and soon after that the First World War started. He voluntarily enlisted in the Canadian Army. He was sent to the war front in Europe. At first Japanese Canadians were not accepted in the Canadian army but when it was realized that Japan was an ally of Britain about 250 Japanese Canadians were enlisted. As it was determined that a Japanese Canadian regiment was not to be formed, the Japanese Canadian recruits were scattered among various Canadian regiments, so Shimbashi did not know what was happening to his friends. At the war's end, he discovered a number of his friends had been killed in action.

In 1923, Zenkichi Shimbashi returned to Japan to be married. As he carried a Canadian passport, he remembered being asked by a Japanese immigration officer in Japan why he had such a passport when he was a Japanese.

After the Second World War Mr. Shimbashi purchased a farm in Barnwell, Alberta. This farming operation subsequently became a huge farming empire of thousands of acres of mixed farming and cattle worth millions of dollars.

Mr. and Mrs. Shimbashi have both passed away leaving their very successful children; Ed, a farmer, Henry, a dentist, Helen and Mae, the first Japanese Canadian nurses in Alberta, Albert, a public relations officer for Turbo resources, Pat, a well known business and sports entrepreneur, William, a provincial civil servant in Toronto and Kathleen, a school teacher in Edmonton.

P. Ichijuro Matsumoto
Ship Builder

In the relocation of Japanese Canadians, one of the greatest needs was that of housing the approximately 9,000 people in the interior ghost towns. In these towns there were only old, dilapidated buildings and unusable hotels. The B.C. Security Commission had to solve this difficult problem and they chose Mr. Philip Ichijuro Matsumoto, a former ship builder from Prince Rupert, to supervise the building of shelters for the Slocan area evacuees. The Slocan area, one of the five main interior camps, was the largest. The others were at Kaslo, Sandon, Greenwood, and Tashme.

Matsumoto and his four sons with a group of carpenters and their helpers went to Slocan and worked extremely hard to repair the hotel buildings and to build new houses. Those of us who lived in these camps during and after the war owe a great deal to all those who helped to build about 2,000 houses under Mr. Matsumoto's supervision.

This remarkable man was born on May 9, 1895 in Tomi-cho, Minami Matsuura-gun, Nagasaki-ken, Japan. His family name was Miura but when he was a child he was adopted by the Matsumoto family and took the family name. After graduating from the eighth grade, he trained as a carpenter and learned to build houses and boats. While still young, he became the manager of his own building enterprise. In 1916, he married Masako Miura. Their first son, Iwao, was born in 1918 and second son, Isamu in 1919. Ichijuro came to Canada alone in 1920 to work for Mr. Suga's boat shop in Prince Rupert. Suga also owned a hotel. Mrs. Matsumoto and Isamu came to Canada in 1924, leaving Iwao under the care of his grandmother.

Later Matsumoto started his own shipyard which became a successful enterprise. They were blessed with three more sons, Tadashi Mark, Judo Luke, and Itsuo John. They were faithful Anglicans and helped the Church wherever they lived. Mr. and Mrs. Matsumoto became naturalized Canadian citizens in Prince Rupert, B.C.

The Second World War changed their lives greatly. Most of the Japanese from Prince Rupert and Skeena River area were moved by railway train to Vancouver. They suffered a great deal of inconvenience and anxiety. All the Matsumoto family except Isamu, were relocated to Hastings Park. Isamu Matthew, born in Japan, was treated as an alien and sent to road camp even though he had just married Mikiko Doi, a second generation Japanese Canadian.

When the Canadian government was planning to set up internment camps, the Japanese Canadian Christian Ministerial Association suggested that the camps be established so that people of the same religious affiliations would be able to live together. This suggestion was accepted and Slocan was chosen as the 'Anglican camp'.

Under I. P. Matsumoto, an earnest Anglican and a successful builder, two types of houses were built in the Slocan area — one type was for single families and another for two families. The two family houses were divided into 3 rooms — one room for each family with a common room in the centre. It was indeed a great undertaking, building 2,000 houses in a difficult situation and in such a short time. The Bay Farm, Popoff, and Lemon Creek camps in the Slocan area were all built by Matsumoto's crew and as well they helped to build the big sanatorium hospital in New Denver.

The Slocan work crew

Mr & Mrs. Matsumoto seated in front of
model of yacht for John D. Eaton former
president of T. Eaton Co.

They were also responsible for supplying water and worked very hard building miles of flumes.

When the war ended the Matsumotos moved to Nelson, B.C., which is situated on the beautiful Kootenay Lake, and soon started building boats again. However, they did not stay here very long for as soon as the government ban was lifted in 1949 and Japanese Canadians were allowed to return to the pacific coast, they moved to Vancouver.

They established the Matsumoto Shipyard Limited on the shores of Dollarton which became a great success. With their honest dealings and fine craftsmanship, they received orders from all over North America. Due to the recent recession many shipyards had to close but the Matsumoto Shipyard has kept on producing. It was on December 4th 1982 that a large fire fighter ship, Pamex 653, was launched at their shipyard. It is said that this ship, built for the government of Mexico, is the largest fire fighter in the world.

Philip Matsumoto and his sons have been extremely successful in their business ventures, but their family have experienced great sadnesses by frequent deaths in the family. First, Iwao, the eldest, was killed in action in Shanghai, China during the Second World War; Tadashi Mark, the third son, passed away while still a youth in Slocan during the war and Judo Luke and his wife, Masako, in 1972. Mrs. Matsumoto, a warm vibrant person, also died. Through all these sadnesses, Mr. Matsumoto's faith in God grew stronger. In 1978 Ichijuro Matsumoto joined his beloved wife.

One of Mr. Matsumoto's hobbies was to cultivate and grow beautiful chrysanthemums. The people of Holy Cross Anglican Church still remember him for on Thanksgiving day every year, he used to offer lovely large chrysanthemums for the altar.

I remember the exceptional warmth and kindness of his personality and his artistic talent in his superb wooden carvings.

Zenichi and Yoshi Kinoshita 1958, in front of Kino's Market in Slocan, store designed by son then attending University of Winnipeg

Mr. and Mrs. Zenichi Kinoshita
Who Lived Thirty Years in a Ghost Town

There is a small town of a half dozen stores and a few hundred inhabitants called Slocan City in the interior of British Columbia. This place was once a booming town with more than five thousand people, most of whom were miners working in the silver mines around the town. Due to the world wide depression and decline of silver value, the mines were closed and many miners left Slocan abandoning their homes and creating a ghost town of old and crumbling buildings. One day to this isolated place many thousands of men, women, and children were sent by the Canadian government. The time was 1942 and the ghost town of Slocan City was suddenly resurrected. The old buildings were fixed and small houses erected for the Japanese Canadians who were uprooted from the coastal areas of British Columbia due to the Pacific War. Many of the Japanese Canadians were sent to places such as Slocan City, Bay Farm and Popoff along the beautiful Slocan Lake and Slocan River areas.

One of the greatest needs of a community is the requisition of food stuffs and with the sudden influx of so many people to the Slocan area a great problem developed. So in order to feed the newcomers several grocery stores were established, one of them Kino's Market which sold meat, fish and general groceries. The operators of this store were Zenichi and Yoshi (Maikawa) Kinoshita. Maikawas owned a similar store on Powell Street in Vancouver before the war. The store in Slocan prospered as they were not only the proprietors of the store but also friends of the Japanese Canadians and local occidental customers.

After the Second World War due to the Canadian governmental policy of dispersing the Japanese Canadians, those who lived in the Slocan area had to leave and go either to Japan or to other parts of Canada, away from the west coast. The place became a ghost town once more. Some of the stores closed down but Kino's Market successfully carried on its business to the few Japanese Canadians who remained in the area and the new 'hippy' community that came to the Slocan Valley. Finally after thirty three years of operating a grocery store in this area Kino's Market was sold in 1974.

The Kinoshitas celebrated their golden wedding anniversary in Burnaby, B.C. on February 23, 1981. In their retirement, they are enjoying travelling, dancing and bowling, Mr. Kinoshita having once in his youth earned his living at a bowling alley. Their travels have taken them as far as Hong Kong where their eldest son Hajime, an architect, and his partner built the Connaught Building, the highest building in Hong Kong.

Takeo Ujo Nakano
Poet

Takeo Nakano was born on September 2, 1903 in the town of Shiida machi, Fukuoka-ken, Japan. From early childhood he was interested in literature and his father taught him to write haiku. As a college youth, he dreamed of emigrating to North America and succeeding in life.

After he graduated from college in 1920, his uncle, a successful strawberry farmer in Hammond, B.C., called him to Canada. Takeo worked on the farm and in winter he cleared the virgin forest. He still remembers the roar that followed the collapse of giant trees, five feet in diameter, felled by two men using a handsaw. The wood was next cut into firewood for the kitchen stove and stacked in a shed. The roots of the trees were dynamited, then burnt using dry leaves and wood. He worked long hours, from before sun rise till starlight. This being his first experience at physical labour, Takeo Nakano remembers waking in the middle of the night, homesick and longing to be with his loving parents. However he summoned his courage and determination and stayed with his uncle for two and a half years.

After his term of service at his uncle's farm he went in October 1922 to work in a pulp mill in Woodfibre, B.C. In 1930 he married Miss Yukie Nishikawa in Japan. Then on March 16, 1942 he was evacuated from Woodfibre and was sent to a road camp in the Rocky Mountains.

He was greatly troubled by the Japanese mill workers' life in camp. They were mostly young, single men who had nothing to do for amusement so they gambled and drank and were rowdy, singing songs and playing the shakuhachi and violin loudly. They often quarrelled and fought before falling asleep on their bunk beds. There were some married people in the town and the single men visited them to buy the illegal home-made wine.

In 1923, there was a flu epidemic in Woodfibre. A young man who was sleeping in the next bed was infected. Takeo told the sick man to wake him up at any time of the night if he needed help. The next morning, Takeo found the young man dead. He felt very sad that the young man had not had the help of a loving doctor or nurse.

About this time a young twenty-four year old man who was an earnest Christian, came from Vancouver to work in the mill. They worked together on the same shift. He was kind and gentle and was eager to convert Takeo to Christianity. A cottage meeting was started one Saturday evening and Takeo was invited. There were six people. For the first time, Takeo heard the Christian gospel and his heart was filled with joy and peace. Another enquirer was added the following week but while they were enjoying singing, two drunken men came in and stopped the meeting. With such incidents and the loss of their leader who had to return to Vancouver, the group faltered. However, Rev. Kosaburo Shimizu and Rev. Zengo Higashi came from Vancouver occasionally and their faith was renewed.

Woodfibre had a Japanese Language School with about one hundred pupils. Mrs. Nakano taught there. The Nakanos were to have two girls, Lily Toshimi and Leatrice Mitsuye.

197

The Woodfibre Japanese had an organization through which they helped each other and the community was peaceful.

With the bombing of Pearl Harbor, the lives of the Japanese in Woodfibre became miserable. On March 16, 1942, some one hundred days after Pearl Harbor, all Japanese males of military age were ordered to go to road camps in the Rocky Mountains. Takeo Nakano will never forget that day. He, the only wage earner for his family, had been ordered to go to Vancouver and thence to the Rockies.

Mr. Takeo Nakano and the other men arrived in Vancouver, and were put into the Hastings Park Manning Pool. After five days' stay, Mr. Nakano was sent to Yellowhead Road Camp at the foot of the Rocky Mountains where there were only boxcars to live in. On March 23, 1942 they arrived in the deep snow with temperatures below zero. The boxcars were spartan. They were forced to work on the maintenance of the highway. He also worked at Descoigne Road camp from April 15 to July 27 when the camp was closed.

He was told that he would be sent to Greenwood, B.C. where his family was interned. He was so happy to think that he could be with his family again. Unfortunately he was not allowed to get off at Greenwood, but was sent to Slocan City from which he was sent to the Immigration building in Vancouver. After three weeks' stay in Vancouver he was sent at the end of August to the prisoner of war camp at Angler, Ontario. He was only able to endure the hardship sustained by his love for his family.

He was released from the prisoner of war camp in mid November, 1943. He and his family were reunited in Toronto after a separation of a year and nine months.

In spite of their hardship, they loved Canada and he was naturalized as a Canadian citizen on December 8th, 1948.

He is well known as an outstanding Japanese poet of Tanka. On January 10th, 1964 he was one of twelve invited by Emperor Hirohito to read their poems and read his tanka, 'Kami'.

As final resting place,
Canada is chosen.
On citizenship paper,
Signing
Hand trembles.

He published a book of poems, Sensei — An Oath, in 1970 in Japan. "Within the barbed wire fence," a prose work, including twenty-one of his poems, mostly written in 1942-43, was published by the University of Toronto Press in 1980. His poems have appeared in Japanese Canadian papers in Toronto regularly almost every month throughout many years. We are all indebted indeed to this talented literary man.

Shigetaka Sasaki
Founder of Judo in Canada

Of the many sports which originated in Japan, such as kendo, karate, and sumo, judo is one of the better known.

One day my dear friend, Shigetaka Sasaki, the founder of Judo Dojyo in Canada and the only person to hold the seventh dan, red and white belt in Canada, visited me. He was then seventy-nine years old but looked much younger than his age. I greeted him warmly and this is what I learned about his life and the judo movement in Canada.

Born at Takamatsu-cho, Sakai Minato Shi, Tottori-ken, on March 1903, Mr. Sasaki came to Canada in 1922. He learned judo in Japan from the founder and great master of judo, Kano Shihan. As a young man, Shigetaka taught judo at Yonago High School and was the Sanin district champion, winning first place for three years running and obtaining the shodan black belt. Although many people urged him to remain in Japan as he was a promising judo-ka and a bright future seemed to be assured him in the Japanese sports world, he chose to come to Canada at age nineteen. When Shigetaka came to Canada, he found some Japanese entertainers imitating judo to please the audience and to make money for themselves. He was very unhappy about this situation and began to do something about it. It took two years of preparation and finally, in 1924 the Judo Club was organized and judo practices were held in Mr. Kanzo Usui's living room at 500 block Alexander Street in Vancouver, B.C. Mr. Ichiji Sasaki, who had a sushi restaurant, was also one of the founding members of his club.

As club membership increased, larger quarters were needed so they moved to a building on Powell Street opposite the Gospel Church, which was then ministered by Rev. Zengo Higashi. Although the fees were only five cents per member, this small amount was not regularly paid by all members. As a result of this, the rental of the hall was covered by Mr. Sasaki. The membership of the club steadily grew and it was constantly necessary to change the club's location. Finally in 1926, the supporters of the club found a big hall at 132 Dunlevy Avenue on the first floor of a hotel. Later they found it necessary to rent all of the main floor. A school with a dormitory was started at the back room of the hall for those students who were financially poor or for those whose parents lived in remote country areas.

Newly arrived students from Japan could not speak English so they were helped by Mr. Saori Goto of the Nikka Yotatsu'Sha, who kindly taught the students to speak English and did not charge any fees. The students paid only for their board. The Judo Club was able to support the school because a kind person had secretly given a large sum of money to the club. Later, they found out that the generous donor was Mr. Etsuji Morii.

In spite of the depression of the 1930s, the Judo Club grew steadily and Shigetaka Sasaki acted as both judo teacher and secretary of the club. Because he was considerate and gentle and democratic in his ways, the Vancouver Judo Club ran very smoothly.

In 1932, the olympics were held in Los Angeles, California, and Dr. Jigoro Kano, one of the Olympic committee members and a master of judo in Japan visited Vancouver on his way to the olympics. Jigoro Kano had changed his Pen name to Kiichi Sai Kano when he reached the age of seventy. Kiichi means "to return to one — the original one or the way." With his permission the Vancouver Judo Club was renamed Kido Kan Judo Club.

On February, 1932, a judo tournament took place. Many notable guests attended such as the mayor of Vancouver, the chairman of the Medical Association of Vancouver, the head of the R.C.M.P., prominent lawyers, businessmen, and others who were interested in and connected with the Japanese community. Mr. Morrow and the Honourable Hachiya were guest speakers at a banquet held after the tournament. The event was a great success.

A few weeks later Mr. Sasaki was called by the head of the R.C.M.P. and asked to start a judo club for them. First they asked for a demonstration of his skill by fighting a boxing champion. It was a strange match, a judo-ka fighting a boxer. However, Sasaki won this interesting contest. Then he was challenged to fight the wrestling champion and again he won the match. About two weeks later, the R.C.M.P. in Vancouver received orders from Ottawa to place judo instructions on the regular course and boxing and wrestling as options. And so Shigetaka Sasaki became a judo instructor to the R.C.M.P., and out of this club eleven members obtained black belts.

Judo became a very popular sport and at tournaments, 300 to 500 fans often gathered. Judo clubs were established at Haney, Mission, Hammond, Wonnock, Woodfibre, Chemainus, Steveston, Kitsilano, Fairview, etc. Shigetaka also had a branch office at the *Vancouver Sun* newspaper. He hoped that through the sport of judo he would be able to soften the anti-Japanese attitude of the paper.

Due to the Second World War, the judo clubs in B.C. were closed and during the war years most of the club members were evacuated to Tashme and later some of them went to sugar beet farms in Southern Alberta, or to Toronto where Sasaki's followers started judo clubs.

In 1956, there was an International Judo Tournament

in Tokyo. Mr. Sasaki went to Japan and through his efforts Canada's Judo performance was recognized and Canada was accepted as a member of International Judo. He retired from his position as the secretary and chairman of the Judo Club of Canada but he is still connected with the clubs in Dunbar, Kerrisdale and West Point Grey in Vancouver. His retirement was March 19 when he was eighty years old.

At present he is trying to write the history of the judo movement in Canada. He explained that he is the only seventh dan received from Kodokan of Japan in Canada. The highest rank is tenth dan. The ninth and tenth dan wear the red belts. The six, seven and eight dan judo-ka wear the red and white belts. The shodan to sixth dan judo-ka wear the black belts.

There are many judo clubs in Canada now and its members are mostly occidental Canadians as the Japanese Canadian population is very small.

Shigetaka Sasaki is enjoying a happy and healthy semi-retired life in Vancouver with his wife. Their only surviving daughter is a school teacher.

Takeo A. Arakawa
Businessman

One day Mr. A. Takeo Arakawa, the chairman of the Board of the Trans-Canada Trading Company Limited, the Tyler Holdings, the Trans-Pacific Fish and the Oversea Courier Service (Canada) visited me. I was interested in Mr. Arakawa's story as he was the manager of the Japan-Canada Trust Savings Company in Vancouver, B.C.

I met the founder of this company, Shinkichi Tamura on board the ship S.S. Fushimimaru in October, 1919 when I immigrated to Canada. Tamura was one of the speakers at a meeting for the passengers of the ship. The meeting was sponsored by the delegates to the first International Labour Congress which was held in Washington, D.C., U.S.A. As a youth, I was greatly impressed by Tamura's story of the hardship he suffered in Canada and the success he later enjoyed.

Takeo Arakawa was born at Kanazawa, Japan in 1904. After graduating from Kanazawa Commercial School in 1923, he was employed in the purchasing department of S. Tamura Trading Company in Kobe, Japan, a company that imported Canadian lumber and fish. He worked in Kobe for three years and in 1926, came to Canada to manage the Tamura Company's Vancouver Branch.

The Tamura Company also operated the Japan-Canada Trust Savings Company in Canada which was called the 'Tamura Ginko' (Tamura Bank) by the Japanese. Arakawa worked for this company until 1935, when he started his own grocery store, the Maple Leaf, at the corner of Dundas and Templeton Streets in Vancouver.

He married Takeko Fukui, a Nisei in 1933 and they were blessed with a daughter, Catherine Keiko in 1940. Leaving the operation of the store to his wife and a hired man, Arakawa worked as the manager of the *Tairiku Nippo* Daily newspaper until the Second World War.

As a result of the war, the Arakawas were evacuated to West Bank, near Kelowna, B.C., in March 1942, where Takeo was employed at an orchard. There were about 150 Japanese evacuees in the Kelowna district and Japanese Canadian children were refused entry into the public school system. Takeo Arakawa, Ken Mori, and Mr. T. Yamada went to the Hon. Bennett, a Conservative M.L.A., in Kelowna for help but they received a cold reception from him. Then, they went to see Mr. Thomas Wilkinson, the president of the Okanagan Fruit Growers' Association, and a member of the C.C.F. party.

"I never knew there were such foolish restrictions in B.C. Do not worry, I will do my best to solve this problem," he said. And within a week Japanese Canadian children were allowed to attend public schools. Mr. Arakawa recalls a number of such incidents where a member of the Co-operative Commonwealth Federation (C.C.F.) party helped the Japanese Canadians, and he said, "It is nice to see there were some honourable and just Canadians who stood up for the democratic rights of all Canadian citizens."

Once, he went to Penticton which is about twenty-five miles south of West Bank to see family friends who were enroute to Greenwood, an evacuation camp. He was detained by the local police and was charged with breaking the law by travelling outside the fifty mile limit of his residence. However, through the authority of the R.C.M.P. detachment at Vernon he was released as it was noted by them that the distance between West Bank and Penticton was less than fifty miles, and it was not Arakawa's intention to stay overnight. He was released and returned home at midnight. Mr. Arakawa stated that the R.C.M.P. protected the Japanese Canadians during the war years.

The Arakawas returned to Vancouver in 1950 and Takeo soon started his own business, the Arakawa Trading Company. His business prospered and at present forty-two people are working in the office and others work in the yards.

Their daughter, Keiko, married Mr. Barry Tyler, who is the manager of the Oversea Courier Service (Canada) Ltd., which handles the distribution of Japanese newspapers and publications in B.C., as well as in the states of Washington and Oregon, U.S.A.

Mr. Arakawa's success in business is due in part to the fact that he worked at Tamura Trading Company which was founded by Shinkichi Tamura, an ardent Christian who believed that honesty and service were the foundation of a successful business. Takeo Arakawa is well known among prominent business people in Japan as an honest and trustworthy person. His company exports lumber and forest products as well as fish to the orient. Now, they have salmon and herring roe and salmon roe processing and cold storage plants at Ucluelet, B.C.

Mr. and Mrs. Arakawa suffered a very sad loss with the sudden deaths of their beloved daughter Keiko, and their two grand daughters, Barbara and Judy in 1978 in an airplane accident. It was a great shock to them. Later Mrs. Arakawa suffered a stroke and although it is very hard to care for a stroke patient, Mr. Arakawa is carrying his heavy duties with cheerfulness and his strong faith in God.

Memories of Kikuno Kitagawa

The following is taken from a story sent by Mrs. Kitagawa, widow of the late Genzo Kitagawa C.M.

My adventures as a young Japanese woman in the unknown world of Canada began in 1926. It was October fourth that year that I married Genzo Kitagawa, at Hikone, Shiga-ken. By December fifth we were aboard the American ship, the S.S. Matheson. I was unable to eat or walk for the first few days from sea-sickness. Huge waves sometimes shook the ship and frightened me or disagreeable oil smells filled the lower decks. But by the time the thirteen day voyage was ended the discomforts were overcome. A Japanese cook on the ship treated us to our surprise and delight with Japanese meals.

On December eighteenth, we arrived in Victoria, B.C. I remember Mr. S. Kuwabara, who had such a hoarse voice, arranging our arrival registration and customs clearance. We stayed over night at the Ishida Ryokan. Since I had come in my kimono, my immediate need was to get new clothing. With Mrs. Ishida's help I went shopping and bought a coat, a hat, a selection of dresses and a pair of shoes from a department store — a totally new experience.

The following day we took a smaller over-night ship and crossed the Georgia Strait to Vancouver. For three days in Vancouver we did some shopping for our new home in Calgary in the Hori-Zen store (Hori is the father of Tom and Bob, who later moved to Regina). I was surprised to find so many Japanese people on Powell Street, and many stores displaying goods imported from Japan. Almost all Japanese goods were available and various services, from hairdressing to banking. I found it interesting to find a store, managed by white people, displaying many kinds of sausages, hanging in a window.

We were aboard the C.P.R. train for a few days and nights and arrived in Calgary. During this trip I had mixed

Genzo and Kikuno Kitagawa , 1973

feelings about this country where our home was to be. What would it hold when the novelty was gone? Anxiety was hidden deep within me. The train travelled into the depths of the mountain, past snowy peaks and forgotten valleys of deep snow. Ghostly blackened trees whispered of a recent forest fire. I wondered then, could there be any village or town at the end of such mountains? My only comfort was to depend on my husband who was leading me into the unknown.

We arrived at midnight, December 19th in Calgary. The city was asleep. We went immediately to the St. Regis Hotel. Early next morning, my husband went to work in a store, the Nippon Silk Co., where he was involved in a business partnership with Mr. Kuwabara and Mr. S. Inouye. About a week later, we moved into a two room suite in Park Hotel which had a small kitchenette and a small bedroom. The public water supply and disposal were across the hallway. The arrangement was far from convenient.

A few days before New Year's day, my husband gave me a sum of money and asked me to prepare for New Year's day. I had no idea of where or how to shop or what was to be done in this strange city of strange customs. My weeping was soundless and helpless, but new friends offered help and we celebrated our first Japanese-Canadian New Year's. From the Japanese families in the city I learned to make miso (soybean paste), and tsukemono (pickled Japanese radishes) using locally available produce.

In 1927, on November 6, around eleven p.m. I was taken to Calgary City Hospital, escorted by Dr. Milan, and an hour later at two minutes past midnight, Mabel Sachiko was born. She was six pounds nine ounces and her healthy cry gave me a feeling of relief and joyful fulfillment. Sachiko was a novelty in this hospital, the first Japanese baby born here. We remained in the hospital for three weeks receiving care and instructions from Mrs. Anneval. Sachiko grew pleasantly, as though accepting of my anxiety. She was named Mabel after an especially kind nurse in the hospital, but when she grew to be a little girl, she did not appreciate the name. We stayed in Calgary for a year and ten months, then moved to Regina on September, 1929. I still have nostalgic feelings whenever I visit Calgary.

In Regina we stayed for two weeks in a rooming house on South Railway and Broad Street. My husband was busy as usual from early morning to late at night, preparing for the opening of the new store. Since there were no kitchen facilities in our temporary rooms, we ate at a nearby restaurant. As a result, Mabel suffered from severe diarrhea and she cried continuously. My despair at the complaints of the neighbours was only eased by the sense that my small child and I were together in our tears and loneliness. It took a few days to arrange for a physician to provide effective medicine to help heal her suffering. I am forever grateful to the young daughter of the landlord, who helped us in our emergency in this totally strange city.

Some weeks later we moved to Moscovitch's apartments, with a suite of three rooms which was large enough for us. The very helpful landlord made us feel as though we'd been released from a prolonged life of suffocation.

About this time, I had a surgical operation from which I recovered without much suffering. Also about this time, Mr. Wakabayashi, in partnership with my husband at the Regina store, went to Japan, married, and returned with his bride to resume his place in this city.

In 1933, we moved to a house on Fifteenth Block on Robinson Street, our first house in Regina. But after two years of severe cold winters we went back to apartment living on Albert Street and Thirteenth Avenue. The following year, Mr. and Mrs. Wakabayashi went to Saskatoon to open their own store, the Mikado Silk on Second Avenue. And, Tom Hori from Vancouver came to help us in our store in Regina.

When Mabel was eight years old, she got the measles. In those days, such cases were isolated in their homes with all members of the household and an order of quarantine was posted on the front door. Previously, there had been a fire in our apartment building — a great commotion with sirens, fire engines and rushing firemen. Mabel in her feverish state recollected the event and whenever her temperature rose, she would suddenly jump from her bed, crying, "Fire! Fire!" and while grasping her beloved doll tightly and a small blanket she would look out the window with a fearful expression, seeing the nightmare through the window. During that time, Mabel was attending Victoria Public School, and often came home with childhood sicknesses.

December 7, 1941, was an unforgettable day for all of us. On this Sunday morning, we remember vividly, the voice of the radio announcer repeatedly shouting, "Japan attacked Pearl Harbour . . ." and later we heard that the United States had declared war on Japan. It was not entirely unexpected, but when it came we realized that we were far from prepared for this emergency. First of all, I wondered if our store should be closed. Next day my husband called all the store employees to discuss this situation but they were very supportive of having the store continue to operate as usual. Only the name Nippon Silk was changed to Silk-O-Lina to avoid unnecessary harrassment from the public.

With the progress of war in Europe and particularly in the Pacific, our feelings of fear for our safety increased. There was an incident of a broken show-window in our store but the damage was slight. We moved from the apartment to a house on Winnipeg Street. One reason was to escape the discomfort of being closely watched by our neighbours. It helped somewhat free our restricted feelings. The war was spreading and with it came a lack of previously imported goods; sugar, tea, coffee, spices, various food stuffs, rubber, oil and its by-products etc. Gradually we moved into the ration supply system and were issued coupon books.

At the same time, there was an unexpected effect on our store business. The mass of people were in a buying mood. Most businesses flourished as did ours and my husband was busy finding suppliers.

A small family like ours was not greatly affected by the ration system. Yet there were times I felt the inadequacy — the empty shelves in stores and the limited choice of products. Our predicament was that rice, our staple food, had disappeared from store shelves. I tried a few grocers from time to time, in various locations in the city but was rarely successful in getting the rice. I often substituted noodles for our supper. All of us Japanese in this city were facing this ordeal together. My husband appealed to the Ration Control Office on behalf of all of us for a fair distribution of rice, as it was our main food. A few days later, as a result of their investigation and an order given to a wholesale distributor, 120 sacks of white rice arrived for distribution in the Japanese community and later we received more rice through the Regina Japanese Club.

During the war years we were somewhat restricted in our movement under the War Measures Act. Both the Canadian born and naturalized citizens were required to report to the local R.C.M.P. station once a month. It was a small restriction, unlike the B.C. Japanese who were forced to relocate from their permanent homes and businesses. However, we were sensitive to criticisms, rumours, and the reactions of people towards Japanese that appeared on the radio and newspapers. In those days Mabel was at the University of Saskatchewan, staying in a dormitory. She graduated in 1950, and later married Tom Tamaki. She has three daughters, Marlene, Brenda and Shelley, and a son, Graham. I have two great grandchildren — a girl Danara and a boy, Daylan.

In 1960, we built our house on McDonald Street beside Wascana Lake. On October 24, 1973 my husband was commended for his service in the community and was made a member of the Order of Canada by Governor-General Roland Michener.

On March 20, 1976, my husband caught a slight cold and was resting in bed for two days when he suddenly passed away at the age of seventy-nine. He left a strong impression on us as a hard worker even to the end.

Mabel and Tom have been very good to me. They took me on an extended auto trip through the Rockies to the Okanagan Valley in the fall of 1976.

I suffered from a broken leg in 1978 and was cared for seven months at the Regina Wascana Hospital. I have been confined to my wheel chair ever since. Even though I was in such a condition I was able to take a holiday trip to Hawaii — thanks to Tom and Mabel and my grandchild, Brenda.

I am now living in Santa Maria Senior Citizens' Home where I am getting excellent care from the sisters, nurses and the staff.

Thomas Kakinuma
Ceramic Artist

There are a number of famous Japanese Canadian artists in the fields of painting, photography, music, literature and ceramics. Mr. Thomas Kakinuma a skilfull, creative and much admired Japanese Canadian ceramicist was one of them.

Thomas Kakinuma was born in Tanuma-shi, Tochigi-ken, Japan in 1908. From early childhood, he liked to draw and so he continued studying to become a painter through correspondence courses from the Tokyo Waseda University until he came to Canada in 1937 at age twenty-nine. He continued to study painting while earning his living at various menial jobs in Vancouver. He moved to Toronto and graduated from the College of Art in 1947. He then went to New York where he studied as a member of the Art Students' League and met the famous Japanese painter, Yasuo Kuniyoshi and learned from him the way to express the beauty of nature in an oriental manner — especially Japanese.

He found it difficult to earn enough money to live by painting so he turned towards the designing and creating of pottery and china. He did not want to give up painting but he became very well known as a good ceramic designer and soon became one of the top ceramicists in Canada. In 1957, he received the highest award in his field, the Grand Art Special Award. His ceramic exhibit was chosen the best out of several thousand exhibits and he earned this honour through working diligently for many years. When this good news reached him, he was overjoyed and shed tears of gratitude to his parents, his native country Japan, and his adopted country Canada. This art exhibit was the most authoritative one in Canada and his fame soon spread all over Canada. In 1959, his two works of art were chosen as the best produced in Canada and were displayed at the Florence Art Gallery in Italy.

The Canadian government recognized his excellence in the arts field and gave him a Canada Council grant which made it possible for him to study for two months in Mexico and eight months in Japan in 1960. While in Japan he studied the famous Satsuma Yaki in Kagoshima and Naniwa Yaki in Miyazaki-ken. He returned to Canada in 1961 and began creating his own unique ceramic wares which were now more polished and beautiful. He won a second prize at the 1962 International Ceramic Exhibit held in Czechoslovakia and he has had fifteen other art shows which were held at Montreal, Toronto, Vancouver, Winnipeg and other places.

Thomas Kakinuma was fifty-three years old when he married Ikuko Kawata, a teacher of the Fujima Ryu Odori (a classical Japanese Dance School). He and his wife were blessed with a daughter. His home life was a happy one and he spent his last years at his home in Burnaby, B.C., creating wonderful works of art and teaching ceramics art at night at the University of B.C. He died at his home on November 2, 1982.

Akiko and Mitsuo Imai
Who Loved Their Community

Many people who live in this vast country, full of small towns and villages do not realize what a wonderful and beautiful country Canada is. We simply live without gratitude nor do we make any effort to show our appreciation, love or concern for the welfare of our communities. However the family of Mr. Frank Mitsuo Imai and Mrs. Akiko Imai showed forth a grateful spirit. They donated eight acres of their precious property to their village in British Columbia. Having visited these friends over many years I can testify to the natural beauty of the land and the generous inner beauty of my old friends.

The following is taken from a dedication speech given by Mr. Imai on the occasion of the public opening of Scotch Creek Ball Park on land which they donated.

President Mr. Myers, Honourable Guests and My Dear Friends:

It is a great pleasure and privilege for my family and me to be here together with you to celebrate the birth of this ball park. It will no doubt play a main role in the physical culture of our community.

At this memorable occasion it is appropriate, I believe, to let you know the background of how this project became possible, and at the same time I would like to ask for your understanding towards the subject.

It was in 1967 I donated the five acres adjacent to the west for the school site in commemoration of Canada's centennial. And now I am glad, having crossed several legal difficulties, to dedicate this three acres officially for the ball park. To many, my actions may give the impression that I am a sort of millionaire but let me call to your attention that I am no relative of the newspaper king, Hearst, of San Francisco. I am a simple hard working member of this community. Let me tell you a little of my hard working life history if I may.

I have been living in Canada for the last forty-six years. At the outbreak of the Second World War, we had to evacu-

Frank and Akiko Imai in front of
twenty-two passenger Imai Express
serving North Shuswap community, 1983

Frank Mitsuo Imai, 1928

ate from Vancouver where we had been living for fifteen years. Actually we Japanese were chased out from the coastal area whether we like it or not. So we went to Celista. The war ended and after our five year stay there we relocated, assisted by friends, to Scotch Creek where we have now lived for the last twenty-six years.

The first few years of our life here was nothing but hard work, clearing very dense forest, felling trees two feet in diameter every day. We planted strawberries as the clearing became larger, first one acre then another acre, and finally we were able to grow strawberries in a five acre field close to this place. But alas, in one winter all our strawberries were wiped out by the severe forty below weather.

In the winter of those years, we used to have much snow and snowdrifts made travel impossible. As a result there were many nights in which people from Celista stayed overnight at our house. The hardship was not only in winter, but early every summer we were attacked by terrible swarms of mosquitoes. It is almost impossible for today's younger generation to understand the hardship of those times. Every now and then I recall our experiences and it is like a bad dream.

We are enjoying a very peaceful life in Canada today, but some troubles exist south of the border. We hear news of Watergate which arouses my curiosity for it seems that a similar situation might have occurred here, since nothing has been done on the school site. However, this current topic of a waterless watergate led me to think of my old days when I created a watergate at Scotch Creek bridge to open an irrigation waterway, digging a long open ditch in excess of two miles, to the strawberry farm. I had to trudge back and forth along the waterway to keep it flowing. Yes, you may even be able to trace the path along the ditch now.

I had thought of moving away when our strawberries were wiped out, but decided to stay on because of the warmth of the friendship we felt. We were rooted here. About that time, some of the Celista young people approached me and asked me to let them use this place to play baseball. I readily agreed. This was about twenty years ago. In those days we had neither electricity nor telephones around here, yet we were contented with our primitive life, and we were very grateful towards the land of Canada. This feeling of gratitude deepens by the day as we live here.

It was about seventeen years ago that the Provincial Park project started on the neighbouring land, and I was fortunately hired for the project. One day the late Rev. Dr. Kosaburo Shimizu, a man for whom I feel the greatest respect and admiration and who was a leader among Japanese Christians across the country, visited us on his way to Vancouver from Toronto. I told him that it had been a long held vision of mine to build a church around here in the future. I was not just trying to please him nor was it merely an expression of impulsive and excited delight due to his visit. He took my story back to Toronto and reported it to the Toronto bi-weekly Japanese newspaper. I have often pictured scenes — those beautiful Christmas scenes of horse drawn sleighs heading towards light streaming through stained glass church windows rich with meaning. Yes, building a church was a heartfelt wish that I cherished for a long time, until yesterday.

But today we have established a temple of physical culture here. Let me say that my dream has come true in a different form. I don't need to remind you that physical fitness is one of life's vital elements — as a wiseman of old once said; "A good spirit dwells only in a healthy body." To promote and encourage sports is to attain just that. That is why physical fitness movements are springing up all over the world. I believe that if we could live with true sportsmanship we would have a beautiful, peaceful and pleasant community.

I would like to add one more thing, and that is that extra effort be made to keep this park beautiful and to utilize it in as many ways as possible. Keeping a place beautiful reminds me of the famous Norwegian explorer, Captain Amundsen, whose motto was: "The things which seem impossible today may become possible tomorrow." With this conviction firmly etched in his mind he reached the

North Pole and then the South Pole as well. He did realize his dream. He lived in a small aircraft cabin during his expeditions and he kept his unusually small home always beautifully furnished. He strove to live a daily life of quality and excellence. In realizing his dream he contributed to the cause of the world's progress. Now jets fly over the North Pole to Europe making quite a short cut. But of course Captain Amundsen is only one of the great men who has contributed to the cause of world progress.

I would like to let you in on a secret. You may be surprised to learn that Captain Amundsen's adopted daughter is living among us. She is Mrs. Vaillancourt. Every time I meet her I think of her father Captain Amundsen, of his adventurous life and his great achievement.

To keep places beautiful has been a part of my life — growing and nursing flowers, particularly tulips. You may recall the beautiful tulips (a hundred dozen of them) decorated annually for the May Queen. I have also given them away to hospitals and for sick people at home.

I am seventy years young, a long ways from a hundred, and am going to have a little rest in our community. It is my earnest prayer that you will have beautiful, strong physiques and at the same time have a wonderful spirit. I ask you to use this park continually and keep it as a beautiful place of your own.

In closing I wish to thank Mr. Myers, Mr. Clark, and many other officials for their untiring efforts in assisting my dreams to come true today. I thank you very much.

Frank Mitsuo Imai

Things change. People come and people go. But the spirit of this pioneer will never die, shining in the beautiful shores of Shuswap Lake, B.C.

Yasutaro Yamaga

Kichinozo Imayoshi

(STORY PAGE 50)
(STORY PAGE 75)

Mr. & Mrs. Takeji Maehara - 1944

Kiyosuke & Kiyoshi Iwabuchi

(STORY PAGE 99)
(STORY PAGE 105)

Koryo Tanaka & E.S. McCadden
at Langara Golf Club - 1927

Chiyo & Iwakichi Sugiyama

(STORY PAGE 122)
(STORY PAGE 135)

Rintaro Hayashi

Shiro Koga - 1959

(STORY PAGE 158)
(STORY PAGE 161)

Teru ~ Seiku Sakumoto

Tsutae ~ Hanako Sato

(STORY PAGE 165)
(STORY PAGE 180)

Takaichi Umezuki

Takeo Ujo Nakano

Mrs. Nakano, heatrice Mitsuye, Lily Toshiemi

(STORY PAGE 185)
(STORY PAGE 196)

Shigetaka Sasaki

(STORY PAGE 199)